About Demos

Who we are

Demos is the think tank for everyday democracy. We believe everyone should be able to make personal choices in their daily lives that contribute to the common good. Our aim is to put this democratic idea into practice by working with organisations in ways that make them more effective and legitimate.

What we work on

We focus on six areas: public services; science and technology; cities and public space; people and communities; arts and culture; and global security.

Who we work with

Our partners include policy-makers, companies, public service providers and social entrepreneurs. Demos is not linked to any party but we work with politicians across political divides. Our international network – which extends across Eastern Europe, Scandinavia, Australia, Brazil, India and China – provides a global perspective and enables us to work across borders.

How we work

Demos knows the importance of learning from experience. We test and improve our ideas in practice by working with people who can make change happen. Our collaborative approach means that our partners share in the creation and ownership of new ideas.

What we offer

We analyse social and political change, which we connect to innovation and learning in organisations. We help our partners show thought leadership and respond to emerging policy challenges.

How we communicate

As an independent voice, we can create debates that lead to real change. We use the media, public events, workshops and publications to communicate our ideas. All our books can be downloaded free from the Demos website.

www.demos.co.uk

First published in 2006
© Demos
Some rights reserved – see copyright licence for details

ISBN 1 84180 163 1
Copy-edited by Julie Pickard, London
Typeset by utimestwo, Collingtree, Northants
Printed by Upstream, London

For further information and
subscription details please contact:

Demos
Magdalen House
136 Tooley Street
London SE1 2TU

telephone: 0845 458 5949
email: hello@demos.co.uk
web: www.demos.co.uk

The Business of Resilience

Corporate security for the 21st century

Rachel Briggs
Charlie Edwards

DEM☉S

DEM☉S

Contents

Acknowledgements

First, we would like to thank our partners, without whose support this research would not have been possible. They are BP, British Airways, Control Risks, E.On, G4S Global Risks Ltd, HSBC, Kroll Security International, Prudential, QinetiQ and Shell.

In particular, we would like to thank Karl Barclay, Alastair Barron, James Cheshire, Graham Clarke, Peter Enzer, William Fell, Richard Fenning, Ken Heap, Nigel Jones, Ron Lindsay, Ian McCredie, Chris Smith, John Smith and John Sullivan.

Many thanks to those who agreed to be interviewed, attended or spoke at seminars, or met with us in India, South Africa and the USA. They are too many to name, but special thanks to Frances Allen, Sanjiv Bhalla, Professor Edward Borodzicz, Barnaby Briggs, David Burrill, David Crow, Les Dauth, Mike Davis, Philippa Foster Back, Peter French, Chris Gentle, Nikki Heath, Chris Holtom, Dan Hooton, Nimisha Iyer, Hamish Macdonald, John Maltby, Francois Marais, Nick Proctor, Don Randall, Sanjay Razdan, David Reece, Tim Reilly, Mark Sanna and Linda Sharpe.

Finally, thanks to the whole Demos team which has offered all sorts of support along the way, but especially to Natasha Barrass, Tom Bentley, Paddy Dewhurst, Sam Hinton-Smith and Tracy Sartin.

Rachel Briggs
Charlie Edwards
June 2006

About the authors

Rachel Briggs is head of international strategy at Demos and runs Demos's Global Security Programme. Her research focuses on the changing domestic and global security environments and how they impact on personal, organisational and national security. It stresses the importance of governments, the private sector and citizens working together to tackle security threats and build resilient organisations and communities. Her current research projects are on counter-terrorism, counter-radicalisation, corporate security, security sector reform, security governance and development, and cultural diplomacy.

She is the author of several reports: *The Kidnapping Business* (2001), *Keeping Your People Safe* (2002), *Travel Advice: Getting information to those who need it* (2002), *The Unlikely Counter-Terrorists* (ed) (2002), *Doing Business in a Dangerous World: Corporate personnel security in emerging markets* (2003), *Healthy Travel: Effective communication to improve travel health outcomes* (2003), *16 Days: The role of the Olympic Truce in the toolkit for peace* (2004) and *Joining Forces: From national security to networked security* (2005).

Charlie Edwards is a researcher on the Global Security Programme. His current work focuses on corporate security, the role of the private sector and non-state actors in security sector reform, and human security issues. Charlie works directly with senior police officers through Centrex, the Central Police Training and Development Authority, and has run training courses with the UK Department for International Development and the Organisation for Economic Co-operation and Development (OECD).

Previously Charlie worked for a political consultancy and in the UK Parliament where he focused on defence and security policy. He began his career working at NATO. Charlie is a research associate at the Centre for Defence Studies and has an MA in War Studies from King's College London. He is the co-author of *A Force for Change: Policing 2020* (Demos, 2006).

Notes on the research methodology

We used a number of research methods during the course of this project. These included:

- O   a literature review and background research
- O   three research seminars in London
- O   fieldwork in India, South Africa and the USA, meeting with heads of corporate security and their teams, people with responsibility for security within business units, other business representatives, security companies, industry bodies and non-governmental organisations (NGOs)
- O   in-depth interviews in London with the heads of security from ten major multinational companies
- O   a survey of 50 security managers conducted on the phone and over the internet
- O   informal discussions and conversations.

This report focuses on multinational companies. There are commonalities between the security challenges facing large companies and small and medium-sized enterprises (SMEs), but there are also many differences. Therefore, while some of our analysis and conclusions may be relevant for SMEs this has not been tested during the course of our research. This is an area that requires much more attention, but is beyond the scope of this project.

Executive summary

Doing business is getting more and more complex. Globalisation has changed the structure and pace of corporate life; the saturation of traditional markets is taking companies to more risky places; the shift towards a knowledge economy is eroding the importance of 'place' in the business world; new business practices such as offshoring challenge companies to manage at a distance; and new forms of accountability, such as corporate governance and corporate social responsibility, put added pressure on companies to match their words with deeds, wherever they are operating. One response has been the **shift from functional to matrix structures**, where companies organise themselves into teams with diverse skills and expertise to solve specific business problems, power is devolved to the local level, and effective management relies on being able to work across the organisation through trusted networks rather than the official channels.

At the same time, security risks have become more complex, too. Many of the threats, such as terrorism, organised crime and information security, are asymmetric and networked, making them more difficult to manage. There is also greater appreciation of the interdependence between a company's risk portfolio and the way it does business: certain types of behaviour can enhance or undermine an organisation's 'licence to operate', and in some cases this can generate risks that would not otherwise exist. As a result, security has a higher profile in the corporate world today than it did five years ago. Companies are looking for new ways to manage these risks and the portfolio of the security department has widened to include shared responsibility for things such as reputation, corporate governance and regulation, corporate social responsibility and information assurance.

As the function comes of age, the corporate security community has been trying to understand **how to align security with the business**, so that doing business and doing security go hand in hand. We have spent 12 months observing multinational companies and have found a handful that appear to be doing this successfully. This report sets out what we have learned about their strategies to allow others to replicate their policies and practices.

These companies understand that the challenge for corporate security is no different from that for any other function – they must keep pace with their company's changing business environment and ensure that how they work, what they do and how they behave reflect these realities.

They exhibit six important characteristics:

1   They understand that **security is achieved through the everyday actions of employees right across the company**. It is not something that the corporate security department can do to or for the company on its behalf and its functional success is therefore dependent on its ability to convince others to work differently. This places emphasis on communication and requires security departments to value the views of non-security professionals just as much as those of the experts.

2   They recognise the **limitations of command and control approaches to change management**. Behaviour is altered only by convincing, persuading, influencing and explaining why a new way of working is in each person's interest. This requires departments to work through trusted social networks, which places greater emphasis on people, management and social skills than security

experience. The power of the corporate security function is now directly proportionate to the quality of its relationships, not the depth of its content knowledge.

3   They understand that **their role is to help the company to take risks rather than eliminate them, and to have contingencies in place to minimise damage when things go wrong**. Risk-taking is essential to successful business and corporate security departments must not behave as security purists whose work detracts from, rather than contributes towards, the company's goals.

4   They **embrace and contribute towards their company's key business concerns**, and as a result are **expanding the security portfolio significantly**. Corporate security departments now have responsibilities in areas such as corporate governance, information assurance, business continuity, reputation management and crisis management, which is causing many to question the relevance of the term 'security' to describe what they do. The term **resilience** now more accurately reflects the range of their responsibilities.

4   They **draw a clear distinction between the strategic and operational aspects of security management**, and have created group corporate security departments to lead on strategy, leaving operational work to be carried out by business units. They all have a clear philosophy to guide their approach to security, which provides direction for non-security professionals, makes it easier to communicate across the company, sell itself to the board, and be credible alongside other functions.

5   Finally, and most important symbolically, the corporate security departments that are leading the way have **abandoned old assumptions about where their power and legitimacy come from**. Their position does not rest on that which makes them different – their content knowledge – but on business acumen, people skills,

management ability and communication expertise. In other words, they have to compete on the same terms as every other function in the company. This is leading many organisations to place greater emphasis on these skills than on a security background and some have people working on security who don't have any security experience at all.

This report highlights a number of practices – some current, others aspirational – which constitute a manifesto for twenty-first-century corporate security.

Philosophy for security

Corporate security departments must:

O   'let go' – they cannot deliver security to the rest of the organisation and must be committed to the idea of commitment-based security; they understand that their authority and legitimacy come from openness and transparency rather than secrecy, and work hard to dispel the 'security myth'

O   not practise the 'dark art of security' – they should not overreact to 'security moments' or use them cynically as opportunities to fight for more resources or authority, nor seek to play others' lack of knowledge to their own advantage

O   be driven by business priorities – from new organising principles, such as corporate governance, to new business practices, such as offshoring

O   not look for Rolls-Royce solutions – absolute security is not possible anywhere, and is certainly not desirable in a corporate setting where the economic imperative is key

O   place a premium on good relationships both within the company and between the company and its stakeholders; fortress security can lose a company friends as well as harm the bottom line

○ understand the importance of communication – they must work hard to sell their services, gain visibility across the company, influence key decision-makers and challenge misperceptions, where necessary.

Group security department

Departments must:

○ expand their work far beyond the traditional security portfolio to include issues such as business continuity, reputation, risk management and corporate responsibility; this creates added pressure to manage across, emphasising the importance of networks and change management skills
○ have as short a reporting line to the board as possible
○ act as a key point of coordination for corporate security (in the widest sense) across the company
○ embrace changes to the internal and external environments
○ understand that there is still more work to be done in aligning security with the business through, for example, strategic plans, metrics that measure the work of the department against the strategic priorities of the business, and more formal links with other parts of the business (for example appraisal processes).

Head of security

Heads of security must:

○ be effective leaders – they should be credible players alongside peers at the top of their companies and have democratic and open styles of leadership within their own teams
○ occupy senior positions within their companies
○ have regular contact with their boards and senior

management teams and invest significant time in raising awareness of security among the board members
o   work at a strategic rather than a tactical level; be presentation-led rather than content-led
o   view their security experience as being far less important than their business, management and communications experience.

Security team

Security teams must:

o   value diversity – gender, age, ethnicity, leadership styles and core competencies
o   place a premium on business skills
o   understand the importance of investing far more time and resources on the mechanisms for change – personnel development, fast-track schemes for security professionals, rotation and developing qualifications.

Organisational structure

Corporate security departments must be committed to business integration, and will achieve this through a number of means, such as:

o   sitting on key committees and working groups that link them into other areas of the business or give them influence at a senior level
o   being committed to alignment with the project management and coordination process
o   developing a variety of reporting structures, with an understanding of the importance of 'structural layering'
o   delegating as much responsibility as possible for security from group level to the business unit
o   valuing the regional layer, but acknowledging that it is difficult to get right; developing innovative responses, such as 'cluster security' models

O   having small central budgets, with the bulk of budgets
     decentralised to the business units.

Achieving alignment between security and the business requires the
function not only to widen its remit to cover more risks, but
fundamentally to change the way it works and relates to the rest of the
business. Those companies that manage this transition successfully
will not just be better equipped to deal with the threats from
terrorism, organised crime or employee theft. The types of changes
we advocate will create significant resilience or adaptive capacity right
at the heart of the business. In an increasingly complex and fast-
moving world the successful companies will be those who can
manage change effectively on an ongoing basis. Aligning security with
the business, therefore, does not merely make companies safer – it is
one of the most important sources of competitive advantage in the
twenty-first century.

1. Introduction

Uncertainty and doubt push the boundaries of management as we know it. The raison d'être for organizations and their leaders has long been to increase control and predictability. Dealing with uncertainty involves growing comfortable with ambiguity and trying to build robustness into choices. Indeed, the flight from uncertainty and ambiguity is so motivated, and the desire to reduce what is fundamentally unknowable to probabilities and risks so strong, that we often create pseudocertainty.
Nitin Nohria, Professor, Senior Associate Dean Director of
Faculty Development, Harvard Business School[1]

Doing business is getting more and more complex. The overwhelming force of globalisation has changed the structure and pace of corporate life; the saturation of traditional markets in Australia, Europe and North America is taking companies to new frontiers in more risky markets, such as Africa, Asia, Latin America and the Middle East; the shift towards a knowledge economy is eroding the importance of 'place' in the business world; new business practices such as offshoring challenge companies to manage at a distance; and new forms of accountability, such as corporate governance and corporate social responsibility, are a recognition of the fact that corporate decisions are of public interest and put added pressure on companies to match their words with deeds, wherever they are operating.

One of the most significant responses to these changes has been the **shift from functional organisation and knowledge bases to matrix structures**. In matrix organisations companies organise themselves into teams with diverse skills and expertise to solve specific business problems, power is devolved to the local level, and effective management relies on being able to work across the organisation through trusted networks rather than the official channels.

At the same time, security risks have become more complex, too. Many of the threats, such as terrorism, organised crime and information security, are asymmetric and networked, making them more difficult to manage. There is also greater appreciation of the interdependence between a company's risk portfolio and the way it does business: certain types of behaviour can enhance or undermine an organisation's 'licence to operate', and in some cases this can generate risks that would not otherwise exist. As a result, security has a higher profile in the corporate world today than it did five years ago. Companies are looking for new ways to manage these risks and the portfolio of the security department has widened to include shared responsibility for things such as reputation, corporate governance and regulation, corporate social responsibility and information assurance.

As the function comes of age, the corporate security community has been trying to understand **how to align security with the business**, so that doing business and doing security go hand in hand. We have spent 12 months observing multinational companies and have found a handful that appear to be doing this successfully. This report sets out what we have learned about their strategies to allow others to replicate their policies and practices.

Many of the companies we spoke to – during seminars, informal conversations and interviews in India, South Africa, the UK and the USA – talked about their frustration at struggling to get the attention of the board, having their recommendations knocked back, or constantly having requests for resources beaten down to the lowest possible level. We did, however, find a small group of companies who are in a much different position. Security in these organisations seems to have found a better 'fit'; it has become part of the corporate DNA and is perceived to be something that makes the company work rather than holds it back. The heads of security at these companies have the ear of the board and senior management team and rarely have their funding requests turned down.

So what is the secret of their success?

What makes these companies stand out is not state-of-the-art security technologies, world-beating anti-fraud procedures or security departments full of ex five-star generals, although some may well have these attributes. Instead, **these companies understand that the challenge for corporate security is no different from that for any other function – they must keep pace with their company's changing business environment and ensure that how they work, what they do and how they behave reflect these realities**. They do not take their lead from terrorists, criminals and hackers – they believe that business imperatives drive security, not the other way around. These departments see their role as being change management rather than enforcement and focus on integrating a security dimension into the way the company does business.

This report argues that the leading corporate security departments exhibit six important characteristics:

1   They understand that **security is achieved through the everyday actions of employees right across the company**. It is not something that the corporate security department can do to or for the company on its behalf and its functional success is therefore dependent on its ability to convince others to work differently. Many companies have placed security 'champions' or representatives in different functions, business units or operating companies to ensure there is a local point of contact who can explain, listen to staff concerns and make sure security policies are interpreted in ways that are appropriate for their setting. They also place significant importance on communication

and appreciate that the views of non-security professionals matter just as much as those of the experts.

2   They recognise the **limitations of command and control approaches to change management**. Behaviour is altered only by convincing, persuading, influencing and explaining why a new way of working is in each person's interest. The business environment is fluid rather than fixed, so change management is an ongoing process rather than a finite project. Corporate security departments, therefore, need to build and work through trusted social networks that place greater emphasis on people, management and social skills than on security experience, and require heads of security to lead in inclusive, not authoritarian, ways. The security community, which so often trades on its secret knowledge, covert contacts and discreet working practices, must come to terms with the fact that its power within a company will be directly proportionate to the quality of its relationships, not the depth of its content knowledge.

3   They understand that **their role is to help the company to take risks rather than eliminate them, and to have contingencies in place to minimise damage when things go wrong**. Risk-taking is essential to successful business and corporate security departments must not behave as security purists whose work detracts from, rather than contributes towards, the company's goals. The new business practice of offshoring provides a good example of how the security function can play a more proactive role for the company, leading on risk management and business development in an integrated way.

4   They **embrace and contribute towards their company's key business concerns,** and as a result are **expanding the security portfolio significantly**. Corporate governance is a key organising principle for companies and successful corporate security departments have recognised that they

have an important role and understand how it relates to that of colleagues. Some are now members of key corporate governance decision-making committees and working groups, which increases their leverage at the top of the company. In a similar fashion, corporate security departments now have responsibilities in areas such as information assurance, business continuity, reputation management and crisis management. Many professionals are beginning to question the relevance of the term 'security' to describe what they do, and feel that **resilience** more accurately reflects the range of their responsibilities.

5   They **draw a clear distinction between the strategic and operational aspects of security management**, and have created group corporate security departments to lead on strategy, leaving operational work to be carried out by business units. They all have a clear philosophy to guide their approach to security, which provides direction for non-security professionals, makes it easier to communicate across the company, sell itself to the board, be credible alongside other functions and develop a clear story about how the security strategy adds value to the company's overall business goals.

6   Finally, and most important symbolically, the corporate security departments that are leading the way have **abandoned old assumptions about where their power and legitimacy come from**. Their position does not rest on that which makes them different – their content knowledge – but on business acumen, people skills, management ability and communication expertise. In other words, they have to compete on the same terms as every other function in the company. This is leading many organisations to place greater emphasis on these skills than on a security background and some have people working on security who don't have any security experience at all.

This report focuses intentionally on current best practice in an attempt to open up to a wider audience the 'secrets of success' of those companies that are leading the way. There is still considerable room for improvement though.

First, **corporate security departments continue to place too much emphasis on their relationships with the board and senior management team**. We argue that these links are important, but unless they build and maintain trusted relationships across the company these relationships will be virtually meaningless.

Second, **further work is needed on the ideal shape of the security function**, and the types of structural configurations most appropriate for companies of different size, geographical reach and sector. As the corporate security portfolio expands, the term itself is beginning to sound out of date, and doesn't encapsulate the function's role. 'Resilience' would better describe both the range of activities being carried out and the way that the function operates across the company, and we would advocate the creation of the position of 'head of group resilience' or 'chief resilience officer' to replace the 'head of security'.

Third, **bringing security to life and making it an integrated part of a company's business practices requires much more effort**. Even the most successful companies we spoke to gave examples of decision-making that had failed to understand and take into account the potential implications for security, where slightly altered actions would have prevented security incidents without compromising business interests or affecting performance.

Fourth, **companies are only just beginning to wake up to the importance of skills diversity within their security teams**. Only a handful of the heads of security we spoke to had any business experience, the majority of staff within the function still come from traditional security backgrounds, and recruitment is done through fairly closed and narrow networks. Although some companies are starting to reverse this trend, movement is slow, and security expertise remains one of the primary criteria for recruits.

Security is one of the few areas of business that describes itself as 'non-competitive'; indeed a large amount of informal benchmarking and ideas sharing goes on behind the scenes. This is because companies understand that corporate security is much more than a private corporate concern; it is also a public good. If our private sector is well equipped security-wise we all benefit, as safer employees, consumers or citizens.

Achieving alignment between security and the business requires the function not only to widen its remit to cover more risks, but fundamentally to change the way it works and relates to the rest of the business. Those companies that manage this transition successfully will not just be better equipped to deal with the threats from terrorism, organised crime or employee theft. The types of changes we advocate will create significant resilience or adaptive capacity right at the heart of the business. In an increasingly complex and fast-moving world the successful companies will be those that can manage change effectively on an ongoing basis. Aligning security with the business, therefore, does not merely make companies safer – it is one of the most important sources of competitive advantage in the twenty-first century.

2. The changing global security context

Over the last five years or so, there has been a growing recognition among companies of the strategic importance of security; in a 2004 MORI poll, 97 per cent said security was of concern to them, with just over half of these saying it was of great concern.[2] Eighty-two per cent said they spend more on security now than they did five years ago, and 57 per cent expect to be spending more in five years' time. Companies seem to appreciate the contribution security can make to overall business concerns. When asked in the same survey whether effective security management would bring benefits to a number of core objectives, the results were overwhelming (see table 1). The same poll shows that a company's security capacity is an increasingly important consideration for investors: 87 per cent of investors feel that if a company fails to deal with a security incident quickly and efficiently it would alter their perception of that company; and in the event of a security breach 61 per cent believe there would be an impact on corporate brand or reputation: half think the share price would be similarly impacted, while just under half (45 per cent) think that customer loyalty would also be affected.[3]

9/11 and the new brand of 'global terrorism' has changed the risk profile of large multinationals. The changing nature of the threat and modus operandi – civilian rather than military targets, desire for mass casualties, the possibility of biological or chemical attacks, the targeting of all things 'western' and the recognition of the value of

Table 1. Impact of effective security management on key business concerns

	Great benefit (%)	Some benefit (%)	No benefit (%)	Don't know (%)
Protection of brand and reputation	74	18	7	1
Being able to reassure staff	69	26	5	0
Being able to recruit/retain staff	26	52	22	0
Protection of intellectual property	44	41	14	1
Maintaining customer confidence	79	14	6	1
Maintaining shareholder confidence	70	23	5	2
Continuity of production or operations	80	15	4	1

Source: *Business Security Survey 2004*, MORI, IPSOS and the CBI in association with QinetiQ

hurting a country politically through its economy – make companies more attractive direct targets and more likely to sustain collateral damage. The bombing at HSBC in Istanbul in 2003 and the attacks on Marriott hotels in the Middle East and south east Asia underline this trend.

Companies are beginning to understand the value of managing the risk of terrorism within the much wider context of 'external agents'. They are increasingly targeted by groups such as the Animal Liberation Front (ALF), local protest movements in particular locations, and anti-globalisation groups. One head of security commented: 'We are not just interested in al Qaida. We are also concerned about the ALF and other activist groups around the world. These are what we call external agents. They feature collectively on the group-level risk register and I have to present to the board once a year on the nature of the threat and our response to it.'

Security moments

It has become somewhat of a cliché to say that 9/11 changed everything, but it did mark an important turning point in corporate security. Terrorism may not be the most important risk facing companies; 65 per cent of the companies we surveyed only ranked it as the fifth most important security challenge facing them, behind crime, IT security, fraud and natural disasters. But 9/11 as an event created a 'moment' (as the collapse of Enron did for corporate governance): it was a shock to the corporate system, which focused minds, worried staff and made boards ask questions about how their security was being managed. Almost one-third of the companies we surveyed altered their approach to corporate security significantly in the light of the terrorist attacks in New York and Washington due to a perceived failure of leadership or response.

The impact of security moments on corporate security

Companies responded to 9/11 in a number of ways. A report from The Conference Board on the impact of 9/11 on corporate security found that many chief executive officers (CEOs) were dismayed to discover that the security function was highly decentralised and widely dispersed through their companies' management structures, making accountability and coordination difficult.[4] As a consequence, many without a group security department created one to act as a point of leadership and coordination for security across the group.

One head of security said: 'There has only been a corporate security function here since 9/11. Before that there was just a security manager in our headquarters in New York.' Departments also benefited from inflated budgets. Just over half (52 per cent) of those surveyed in the USA enjoyed permanent increases post 9/11 and 47 per cent had higher staffing levels. The biggest increases were concentrated in large multinationals and companies in critical industries, which are perceived to have the highest exposures to risk.[5] This is consistent with our survey, which showed that over 60 per cent of companies increased security spending post 9/11.

For others, 9/11 highlighted weaknesses in their security set up. In a 2004 MORI poll, 63 per cent of companies said 9/11 had strongly influenced changes they had made to corporate security.[6] Companies revisited their security, business continuity and crisis management plans, everything from their fire drills and evacuation procedures to their training manuals and guidelines and communicating with staff. One of the key lessons of the July 2005 bombings in London was around communication with staff.[7] One company we spoke to realised it did not have a clear incident management plan, and created a new group-level department to drive and own central policies such as these. Another head of security was brought in after the board felt his predecessor had failed to lead. He said: 'During my recruitment process it became obvious that the board was looking for someone more strategic who could introduce a proactive and joined-up approach. The old department had failed to respond to 9/11 and didn't seem to be able to change the way it worked in response to the new security environment.' Interestingly, our survey found that post 7/7 companies had not increased security spend or staff head count, suggesting that they had made the necessary changes after 9/11.

Changing perceptions of security

9/11, like all security moments, was effective because it changed perceptions more than reality. Corporate security departments cannot manage security in a vacuum, detached from the perceptions of staff, the board and wider stakeholders. As one head of security put it: 'Managing perceptions rather than realities is a constant pressure. We have to deal with misperceptions and a lack of understanding; that is part of the landscape for the corporate security department.'

Public perceptions are often at odds with reality. Academic Paul Slovic argues that people tend to make judgements about risk based on emotional feelings and intuitions about whether something is good or bad rather than a dispassionate calculation of costs and benefits, highlighting the importance of images, metaphors and narratives in shaping perceptions.[8] Many academics and scholars have argued that there is a tendency for individuals to assume that an event is more likely to recur if it is easy to remember.

Given the graphic nature of some of the media reporting of security risks in recent years – especially the human suffering of terrorist attacks – and the arrival of 24/7 news coverage, it is not surprising that we worry about terrorism even though the risk of dying in a terrorist attack is dwarfed by the risk of death on the road or in the home. It is also understandable that fears about chemical and biological attacks, for example, have caused anxiety in corporate America. One company we visited in New York had gone as far as investing 'well over a million dollars' in an early warning system in case of a chemical or biological attack and stockpiled vaccinations for its 7000 staff. It is difficult to see how this type of response could be aligned to genuine business interests and is an example of what W Kip Viscusi calls 'zero risk mentality'.[9]

Responding to security moments

Leading security departments share two common features in the way they respond to 'security moments'. First, they resist the temptation to overreact or use them as opportunities to assert their authority. They recognise that overplaying their hand costs them credibility in the long term. Second, they play a proactive role in challenging staff misperceptions through open channels of communication. Corporate security departments have access to considerable amounts of analysis and data on security threats and the companies we spoke to had developed mechanisms for disseminating this as widely as possible, recognising that timing is key. One head of security said: 'My job is to give assurance. Assurance is key to corporate security, giving a sense of safety to the company and its people.'

Accurate information does not just help to calm fears. Everyday decisions about security are not made by the corporate security team, but by staff right across the company. If they do not have a balanced view of the threats, their impact on the company, and what they can do themselves to manage them, they are more likely to behave in ways that undermine rather than reinforce the company's corporate security strategy. An approach to security that rests on the active engagement of staff is sometimes referred to as 'commitment-based security'.

While some companies have – rightly or wrongly – responded to 9/11 and the new security environment, many have not. In the 2004 MORI poll 60 per cent of companies admitted residual concerns about their organisation's state of preparedness and levels are even higher among small businesses (70 per cent).[10] Almost one-quarter (23 per cent) mentioned business continuity and the fact that plans put in place have not been tested; the same proportion were concerned about their ability to detect and respond to threats; one-fifth thought their plans were somewhat inadequate; and 15 per cent were concerned about their vulnerability to IT attacks. The practices showcased in this report are far from typical of the state of preparedness of the business community as a whole.

3. Corporate governance

The new organising principle for corporate security

The rise in regulation, regulated self-regulation, guidelines, protocols and codes of best practice is in part a response to a series of high-profile, high-impact corporate failures, such as Enron, Tyco and WorldCom, that have undermined trust in companies. The proportion of UK citizens who say they have faith in corporations has plummeted, from two to one in favour in 1970 to two to one against today. This erosion of trust matters. As Ciancutti and Steding argue: 'Any organisation in which people earn one another's trust, and that commands trust from the public, has a competitive advantage. It can draw the best people, inspire consumer loyalty, reach out successfully to new markets, and provide more innovative products and services.'[11]

The past decade has witnessed a flurry of activity which is bringing corporate security to the heart of corporate decision-making: corporate governance codes have been published in 43 countries, the OECD, World Bank and International Monetary Fund have produced their own guidelines and there has been a steady succession of committees and reports in the UK, the most notable of which – the Turnbull Report[12] – requires publicly traded companies to report on risks and risk management strategies in their annual reports.

The 2002 Sarbanes-Oxley Act (SOX) covers issues such as establishing a public company accounting oversight board, auditor independence, corporate responsibility and enhanced financial disclosure.[13] Basel II is a set of recommendations from the Basel Committee on Banking Supervision which covers the governance of loss.[14] The committee breaks down loss events into seven general categories, many of which are now within the remit of corporate security: internal fraud, external fraud, employee practices, workplace safety, clients, products and business practice.

Managing security within a corporate governance framework

As companies become increasingly aware of the interdependence between security risks and operating practices, security and corporate governance have converged. One head of security said: 'One of the most important business drivers impacting on security is corporate governance. Security has taken a much bigger role in this, and I now share responsibility for it with the head of group audit and the company secretary.' Many argue that managing security within a governance framework has been helpful in achieving compliance from colleagues and visibility across the company. As one head of security commented: 'Have corporate governance developments helped security decision-making? Yes, they have helped. When we created our corporate governance package we didn't have to write new policies because we already had good ones in place. The problem at that stage was getting people to comply with them. It now works extremely well. The policies are now more visible at senior levels than they were previously. I get a greater level of assurance than I was doing before.'

This is having an impact on the shape and role of the corporate security department. First, it now has a much wider range of responsibilities. A recent report on so-called 'convergence' argues that corporate governance is one of five factors that mean that the corporate security department is now responsible for a wider range of risks, including fraud, corruption, negligence, information security and assurance, money laundering, business continuity planning, regulation, employee conduct, and the response to major events including natural and man-made disasters.[15]

These five factors are:

○ *Rapid expansion of the enterprise ecosystem.* Enterprises are becoming more complex in a global economy where external partners are increasing (eg outsourcing).

○ *Value migration from the physical to information-based and intangible assets.* Increasingly, value is shifting from physical to information-based assets.

○ *New protective technologies blurring functional boundaries.* Emerging technology is creating an overlap between physical and information security functions.

○ *New compliance and regulatory regimes.* More regulations are developing in response to new threats and business interactions.

○ *Continuing pressure to reduce cost.* Enterprises are constantly trying to mitigate risk efficiently.

Second, corporate governance allows the corporate security function to 'play' at an organisation-wide level. The leading corporate security departments report to their boards or audit committees on a regularly, and some now sit on highly influential committees and working groups such as the Resilience Risk Management Committee, the Group Operational Risk Committee, the Operational Risk Management Group and the Security Risk Council. One commented:

Probably the most important committee in which group security is involved is the Group Operational Risk Committee, which is made up of the group chief risk officer, group finance director, group legal services director, head of group risk, group operational risk manager, head of group compliance, head of group security and the risk directors for each of our businesses, with the head of group (internal audit) in attendance. This is a powerful committee because it is able to review risks in any of the businesses or across the group, and ask risk owners, no matter how senior, to provide reassurance that risks have been considered and managed.

Crime: the limits of corporate governance

Although corporate governance has helped to raise the profile and influence of security there are still areas where the function struggles to get the support it needs. In a 2005 report from The Conference Board,[16] security directors ranked theft, fraud and financial crime as the third most important security threat facing their company, and among the companies we spoke to 60 per cent mentioned some form of crime as being the most important security threat to their company.

And yet, most companies do not know the true extent of the criminal threat they face, partly due to poor internal reporting of incidents; fraud and other forms of organised criminal activity have only recently begun to be managed coherently at the group level.

The information gap is perpetuated by senior level apathy. Some companies admitted that it is hard to get their boards to take crime seriously. One head of security who is fighting to get fraud onto the boardroom agenda said: 'The corporate security department thinks fraud is an issue, but if you spoke to most senior executives they would probably say that we should spend less time and money on it. In a company of this size people are happy to just let things go below a certain threshold. Officially we have found $4–5 million worth of fraud, but we have no idea how much of the total we are seeing. We have now put in place a global reporting regime for fraud, and hope we can use the data we generate to strengthen our case.'

Losses sometimes remain hidden because local managers want to cover up their problems. One head of security spoke of his frustration at finding out that something has happened too late to be able to do anything about it, recover any of the losses or learn vital lessons: 'In a global company there will always be local managers who want to keep their problems quiet. We need to educate people about the need to make decisions collectively.'

In some cases there are genuine conflicts of interest between fraud prevention and other business priorities. Fraud loss work often clashes with customer complaints procedures because controls tend to inconvenience customers; the complexity of IT systems can hinder the effective integration of fraud prevention measures; and there can be clashes between crime prevention and sales. One head of security said: 'Sometimes we don't help things by the inconsistency of the messages internally about contraband. We still rate performance on volume sales. On the one hand we say we shouldn't sell to people moving into markets we don't want to go into, but we constantly put pressure on them to increase volume.'

The challenges of corporate security within a corporate governance framework

As understanding of the impact of corporate governance on corporate security is beginning to deepen, concerns have been voiced about the way in which guiding principles are applied in practice. There are fears that overzealous corporate governance could undermine rather than strengthen a company's ability to manage security risks.

Corporate governance has helped to create a culture that supports the furtherance of good and best practice, where information about the most effective types of behaviours, processes, structures and protocols is shared. Security professionals often describe what they do as 'non-competitive' and rely on regular contact and intelligence pooling with peers in other companies to get their jobs done. This mostly happens informally through networks such as the Risk and Security Management Forum (RSMF) and the International Security Management Association (ISMA), or through sector or ad hoc groupings. Inevitably, heads of security often have access to sensitive information about other companies, sometimes competitors, which is governed by a 'gentleman's agreement'. Although no one could recall an instance of this code being broken, it is possible that this code might be considered contrary to traditional approaches to corporate governance.

There is also a danger that corporate governance reinforces the misperception that all risks can be managed away. The corporate security function should avoid the temptation to exaggerate the extent to which it can deliver solutions, which would ultimately reduce the credibility of the function and hinder a company's ability to make the necessary and difficult choices between competing priorities. The current climate of fear also makes it difficult to open up discussions about the law of diminishing returns relating to security spending. As one senior business executive noted: 'There is only so much we can do to prevent a determined agent. There is a grey area as far as expenditure is concerned between enforcing primitive security and creating Star Wars-like barriers.'

The foundation of effective security is trust, and there is a danger that over-formalised and rigid approaches to security undermine rather than reinforce trust. The most important trust relationship for a company in managing its security is with its own staff, which is responsible for delivering security in practice. One senior executive said: 'Rather than doubling the height of a fence around our plants, we have found that a far more valuable expenditure has been to make security increasingly a shared accountability for all our employees. Security is something we all play a part in enhancing, as opposed to it being something that is done to you by a small security team.'

Corporate governance as an organising business principle is here to stay and those corporate security functions that embrace it and help to shape its future development will put themselves at the heart of their companies and will align their work with the pre-eminent business concern of the day. But at the same time, they must do so in a way that strengthens trusted relationships across the company, empowers individual members of staff and does not exaggerate the extent of the risks faced by the company.

4. Good relations

Delivering corporate security through community partnership

*If local people see us as being part of their community they are
far less likely to attack us.*

Head of group security

A company's position within its 'operating ecosystem', its operating
principals and its relationship with local communities and
stakeholders have direct and indirect impacts on its security and its
ability to do business in a sustainable way. Achieving 'peaceful co-
existence' relies on companies having a comprehensive understanding
of the places in which they operate and effective communication
channels with their local stakeholders; the right management processes and structures to encourage and reward relevant behaviours
among their staff; and investing in their local workforce. A company's
social footprint is intimately linked to its corporate security strategy
and the companies that form partnerships between security and
corporate social responsibility are better able to align security with
the business.

Acceptance strategies

When companies are properly integrated into the communities
within which they work they become a partner rather than a target.
Companies could learn a lot from the ways in which non-
governmental organisations (NGOs) manage their security, based on

'the security triangle',[17] which has three elements: acceptance, protection and deterrence. The most interesting section of the triangle is the acceptance strategy, which works on the assumption that genuine security is achieved only when an organisation's work is accepted by the local community. If it understands and believes in what you are doing you are less likely to be targeted. In rare cases, organisations such as the International Committee of the Red Cross have achieved a special 'protected' status, and many more are able to operate with relatively little physical security in place.

Although developed for the NGO sector, the security triangle has relevance for companies, and can be used to good effect by those who have a proper understanding of the local environment and their impact on it. Achieving this type of approach in practice relies on a long-term, sustainable business strategy underpinned by changed business practices and a set of sound operational values. It is at odds both with short-term 'market plunder' approaches to doing business and heavily defensive security measures. To achieve this vision, companies must change the way they view threats and challenges and shift from a 'defensive fortress' approach to security to one based on openness and integration.

A company's security is threatened when communities do not see any kind of personal or collective positives from their presence. This is especially – but not exclusively – true in the developing world where the contrast between rich multinationals and their expatriate staff and locals can be stark, such as in countries like Nigeria. The consequences of escalating grievances can be wide-ranging and extreme: companies mentioned reduced staff morale due to verbal abuse; increased staff stress; elevated security costs; community liaison staff fearful of venturing into the community; harmful stories appearing in the local media; internal company gossip; physical abuse of staff; diversion of management time; theft of materials and vehicles; dispute 'creep'; increased scrutiny by regulators; contractors reluctant to provide services; occupation and/or business inter-ruption of facilities; sabotage of facilities; hostage-taking (in extreme environments); law suits and out of court settlements; and harmful stories in the international media, leading to customer boycotts and related effects at group level (for example, reduced share price, higher risk ratings for finance, staff recruitment problems and increased insurance costs).

Secure and sustainable operating environments

Companies cannot take on the governance challenges of the countries in which they operate, but they can contribute towards capacity-building. The factors that frustrate locals – from corruption and poverty, to exclusion and loss of land or resource rights – can also make it difficult for companies to operate, so by working together they can tackle their shared problems, and build important relationships with stakeholders. In increasingly competitive markets, being a 'partner of choice' can be a major selling point for companies, and good relationships can generate useful intelligence about the situation on the ground. As Peter Sutherland, chairman of BP, has said: 'I believe that it is part of building good sustainable businesses to help establish safe, secure, stable and peaceful societies. Business thrives where society thrives.'[18] Companies cannot act as governments, but they can be catalysts for improved governance. This is not an easy or straightforward task for the private sector, not least because companies are unlikely to see the benefits within the contractual lifetime of most project managers, but it will contribute towards their own security and the future stability of their markets.

Building relationships is not a risk-free activity, especially in less stable markets, where corruption, violence and crime are widespread. In such places, companies need to walk a fine line between engagement and keeping a respectful distance, while always being sensitive to the local circumstances, customs, practices and politics. There is a delicate balance between 'coercive engagement' with stakeholders and 'constructive dialogue'.

One company representative shared his experiences of the unintended consequences of stakeholder engagement without sufficient awareness of the local environment. A local restaurant owner who lived opposite the company's site was invited into the facility for a discussion as part of the company's 'stakeholder engagement' process. After leaving the facility, she was approached by a group of armed men demanding money from her, believing she had been bribed by the company. She had of course not been given anything, and the men burnt her restaurant down when she was unable to pay. While the project managers had been keen to engage with the community and had entirely positive intentions, they had not taken on board the potential outcomes of their actions, in a country where corruption and bribery were widespread.

Know your neighbour

Companies need a comprehensive understanding of the places in which they operate, and the customs of local communities. Even with the best of intentions, not knowing your neighbours can get you into trouble. One company described its operation in the USA, where local managers were fully signed up to stakeholder engagement and took the views of local communities very seriously. Every year they paid a company to conduct local telephone surveys to gauge attitudes towards their presence, which consistently generated 90 per cent approval ratings. They were therefore shocked when there was a sudden outbreak of opposition, as it seemed out of touch with their understanding of local perceptions. They then realised that their phone surveys were far from representative; African-American households had proportionally far fewer phones and they were failing to reach some of the most marginalised and vulnerable within their local community – those with the most potential for grievance.

BP has trialled some innovative work in Venezuela. In the late 1990s, BP began exploration work in the Orinoco Delta region of the country, an area traditionally inhabited by an indigenous group called the Warao. To gain a better understanding of the Warao, an external expert was commissioned to write a report summarising their history, lifestyle, social structure, language and religious beliefs. The report assisted BP in understanding key aspects of the Warao, including areas in which they were most likely to be vulnerable to BP's activities as well as priority areas for support. It was then able to adapt its plans to cause the least amount of impact. In addition, as an 'introductory text' on the region and its peoples, the report was also widely distributed to BP personnel to improve their understanding of the community alongside whom they were living and working. BP is, interestingly, one of the few companies that has brought together security, communications and community relations under a single line of management to encourage coherence between these three strands.

Communication

The starting point for good community relations is effective communication and our research has revealed a number of key lessons for companies. First, they should remember that good communication starts with good listening to ensure they understand the issues and interests of the people they want to talk to. And all subsequent communications should incorporate some form of feedback mechanism. Second, it is vital to use a wide variety of communications tools; one size never fits all, and they should ensure their chosen mechanisms are locally acceptable. Third, companies should see communication as a long-term commitment, with individual efforts to be repeated in a timely and regular fashion, as necessary. They should, of course, also recognise that openness and transparency minimises the possibility of confusion both internally and externally, and make sure that messages are consistent with and supportive of one another; they shouldn't assume that communication intended for one audience won't be seen by another. Finally, companies should be cautious of over-committing and under-delivering; as a number of the companies we spoke to noted, local communities can have very long memories, stretching far beyond the career lifespan of most project managers.

A multinational company working with a national development and regeneration agency in Peru provides a good example of how companies might go about communicating with stakeholders. The region they were working in is particularly rich in natural biodiversity and has large numbers of indigenous people. Their communications objective was to help establish positive relations between the company and the local communities by explaining the project, addressing fears about health, safety and environmental risks and raising awareness of the mitigation, compensation and social investment programmes they had established. The company used a variety of communication tools:

O   two- to three-monthly briefing papers addressing
     environmental and social issues including a feedback
     section
O   regular letters signed by the health, safety and
     environment manager to indigenous communities to
     observe protocol and personalise contact
O   independent third-party reports on local conditions
O   education programmes and capacity-building, such as
     public health information, supplied in local languages
     with easy-to-understand pictures
O   copies of environmental, social, health and safety impact
     assessments were widely distributed, including non-
     technical summaries
O   health and solar power information specifically designed
     to communicate to the local peoples (printed on paper
     that would not rot in the jungle).

Formal partnerships

In some cases, companies go as far as to develop formal partnerships with local communities as a way of developing trusted relationships. Companies that develop local business to support themselves and the local community find they begin to create a more benign and secure environment in which to work. One initiative in South Africa that brought together a major company and a number of local enterprises has seen a high success rate in community regeneration. With the support of the company a new laundry was opened in August 2004 in South Africa. Klein Begin Laundry has already expanded twice, and has created five full-time and three part-time jobs, all for formerly unemployed people. While the immediate effect is small, the use of local business has had a knock-on effect in the wider community. This initiative demonstrates how companies should not rely solely on philanthropic donations, but use their core business competencies to have a local impact.[19]

Internal support mechanisms

Companies must also ensure this work is supported and reinforced by appropriate internal processes. Staff members are the main contact between the company and the community so it is crucial that they understand the company's long-term objectives within each locality, and how their behaviour will impact on them. Having an in-house champion can help: someone who can drive the approach internally, ensure management and staff buy-in, find a staff member or facilitator who has time for the leg-work, and find the right community partners. This must be underpinned by incentive and management structures that support behaviours that do not reward violent behaviour; convey disrespect for stakeholders; decrease security and quality of life; lead to fragmentation; or reduce the capacity and willingness of authorities to provide services or their capacity to commit violence.

One of the main limiting factors is the project management timeframe. Many managers are on short-term postings (one to two years) and are under pressure to deliver results quickly. Companies need to shift their working practices to make community engagement the cornerstone of good project management and allow time at the end of postings for managers to pass on their community networks to successors.

Companies must also ensure they invest in their local workforce. The lack of training and opportunities and high staff turnover were all identified by companies as being part of the 'security' problem; when staff do not feel valued they are less likely to respect their employers, and rates of theft and absenteeism tend to increase. This type of investment also influences the extent to which companies are subject to more diffuse forms of grievance. One company noted that after one of their worst-performing operations had been hit by a major incident the company invested in counselling for all employees. Subsequently, the rate of theft and absenteeism decreased and productivity at this poorly performing operation rose significantly.

Community-based corporate security

There are clear links between the way a company does its business, the quality and depth of its relationships with the community, and its ability to operate in a safe and sustainable way. Its approach to security and risk management is part of this picture, and there are a number of ways in which the corporate security function can have a positive and tangible influence.

First, the corporate security function needs to achieve clear and close alignment with the project management process. Project managers operate at the front end delivering this strategy and are essential to its success. If they do not buy into the idea that companies and communities work together to deliver safe, secure and sustainable environments, it will never come to fruition. Corporate security professionals can also gain substantially from this relationship; anecdotal evidence suggests that information gleaned from the most innocuous meetings between project managers and local communities can be highly relevant to security managers.

Second, the group security department needs to position itself within group level discussions about corporate social responsibility, social performance and community relations. As the debate about community engagement develops from bolt-on philanthropic activities to changed business practices it is important that the security department understands what it can contribute to and gain from its involvement in this area of business activity. This shift presents a window of opportunity for corporate security departments to find effective ways of collaborating on projects that focus on developing relationships with the community, with an understanding that this can lead to enhanced security.

Third, the corporate security function must discourage 'fortress' approaches to security management. Bad security can lose a company friends; security strategies that are defensive and aim to build barriers are more likely to have a negative impact on a company's relationship with local communities and create more problems in the long term. What's more, using disproportionate measures to counter expressions of community grievances will also have an adverse effect on community relations and do nothing to strengthen the company's position.

5. Offshoring

A new role for corporate security

The picture that is emerging is one of a corporate security function operating at the heart of corporate life, with a greatly expanded portfolio of responsibilities and an ability to influence the way a company operates. The role of corporate security in offshoring offers an excellent example of this approach in practice. Due to the perceived and real security risks in countries such as India, Indonesia, Malaysia and the Philippines, the corporate security function has tended to play an important role in the planning and delivery of offshore operations. Little of what it has done relates to 'traditional' security concerns, but rather to business continuity, information assurance, human resource risks, regulation and reputation management. Offshoring provides a good illustration of the ways in which the corporate security department can collaborate horizontally across the company as well as globally around the world, playing a front-of-house and business development role.

The rise of offshoring
Offshoring is generally defined as moving part of a company's operation abroad either to 'a captive', ie a wholly owned subsidiary or a joint venture.[20] It is not to be confused with outsourcing, which involves a company subcontracting part of its work to a third party, which takes place both at home and abroad. Much offshoring activity takes place in India, which is regarded as the offshore capital of the

world. It is largely focused on Bangalore and Mumbai, but attention is shifting rapidly to other cities such as Chennai, Delhi, Hyderabad, Kolkata, Mangalore and Pune.

There are no comprehensive statistics about offshoring, but one research institute in the USA estimates that 3.3 million jobs will move offshore by 2015, while others estimate that as many as six million US jobs will migrate overseas in the next decade.[21] The Indian government has forecast that the country will need one million trained and qualified call centre workers by 2009, but by that time about a quarter of those positions will remain unfilled.[22]

The initial rationale for offshoring was financial: lower labour costs make doing business much cheaper. Companies have not had to trade quality for cost. India, for example, produces 2–2.5 million graduates each year, more than 80 per cent of whom are English speakers.[23] A large European insurance company recently found that moving part of its operations offshore improved 'keying' accuracy from 84 per cent to 96 per cent,[24] so it is not surprising that large companies are moving a growing proportion of their operations offshore.

Companies are beginning to move more complex business operations such as research and development abroad. Only one in every ten pounds is spent on call centres, with the remaining nine pounds spent on a myriad of different business operations including payroll processing, data entry, insurance renewals and some IT operations. For example, AstraZeneca (AZ) recently opened a multimillion dollar research facility in Bangalore, its CEO, Sir Tom McKillop, explaining that the decision had been based on the quality of Indian scientists.[25]

The political and security risks of offshoring

The bombings in Delhi in 2005 are a reminder that the political situation in India remains fragile. The Indo–Pakistan conflict continues to rage, and as a result political risk remains an obvious concern for companies operating within the region. From 2000 to 2003, the US State Department's 'Patterns of Global Terrorism' report recorded 203 international terrorist attacks in India,[26] the vast majority of which were related to the conflict in Kashmir. The car bombs that killed 52 people and wounded more than 150 in Mumbai in August 2003 were a clear signal that the focus of attacks is no longer Kashmir itself, but India's urban areas. In March 2005 Indian police shot dead three men and arrested two others who were allegedly part of the Lashkar-e-Toiba group that was planning an attack on leading software firms in Bangalore.[27]

As large multinationals relocate many of their core development functions to offshore sites, there is a danger that these operations are vulnerable to terrorist attack. Groups seeking to target financial institutions might prefer to carry out their attacks in places like India where law enforcement and intelligence capabilities are lower and where companies are therefore more exposed. Some companies considered part of the UK's critical national infrastructure, such as utilities, communications, defence and so on, have privately expressed concerns along these lines. For example, one defence company said it is worried that it has outsourced part of its business to a company which is now planning to move offshore within the next few years, further weakening the controls set in place at the start of their agreement. During interviews and meetings both in the UK and India some companies confided that they are reassessing their offshoring operations, concerned that they have let go of too many critical functions that should be brought back to the UK for security and business continuity reasons.

However, with the exception of Assam, Jammu and Kashmir, Manipur and Nagaland, most areas of India do not experience high security risks, and most companies, their staff and operations will experience little more than petty crime and low level corruption.

People problems

As in the UK, risks for companies at their offshore operations are just as likely to be internally as externally created, making it important that companies do not overlook the potential risks posed by their own staff. Our research suggests that companies are actively managing this risk.[28] We observed a range of security measures, from swipe cards, security guards and random searches to CCTV and airport-style detectors. Staff do not normally have access to the internet, email or printers, and all personal belongings are stored in lockers away from sensitive areas.

Given the level of security procedures in place there is no evidence to suggest that consumer data is at greater risk in India than in the UK.[29] Even those companies considering relocation did not cite these types of security breaches as the main concern, but rather the complexity of responding to an incident at an offshore operation. Nevertheless, even a suggestion of a breach could cause considerable concern and result in reputation damage. In response, the National Association of Software and Service Companies (NASSCOM), the Indian trade body, has suggested creating a nationwide database of call centre staff with security clearance, which employers would pay to access.[30]

High staff turnover is a growing disruption for companies with offshore operations in places such as India. The exact scale of turnover is difficult to measure, but some commentators estimate it would be more than 40 per cent per year.[31] During meetings in India, companies admitted to having attrition rates of anything between 15 per cent and 50 per cent. As a result, many have developed activities such as motivational programmes for staff and industry-wide initiatives pioneered by NASSCOM. Some companies are entering into 'no poaching' agreements with each other, and adhering to a NASSCOM-promoted code of conduct that urges companies not to employ people who have not served their full notice period or are persistently 'job-hopping'.[32] The growing pool of graduates means there is no shortage of willing potential employees though.

The level of staff attrition has a detrimental impact on the growth of a company's organisational culture. Successful offshoring requires companies to acquire the ability to manage a multicultural environment and build a global corporate culture.[33] This is difficult enough in places like India, but is exacerbated by the high turnover of employees. Corporate culture is a key determining factor in the relative success of corporate security. Those companies that are unable to build tacit and explicit shared understanding of the rationale for security and the role of the staff will find it difficult to build secure workplaces in practice. Stability is an important element in corporate security policy and practice.[34]

Environmental and infrastructural challenges

The floods of July 2005 in the Indian state of Maharashtra, which includes Mumbai, were the eighth heaviest floods on record. Approximately 37 inches of rain fell in a 24-hour period, leaving at least 1000 people dead, the airport closed, telecommunications paralysed, and public transport at a standstill. Doing business in places like India is impossible without solid contingency plans in place. One head of security noted that their decision to site their operations on high ground at extra cost had paid off as they had been relatively unaffected by the flooding, unlike most of their competitors, who had experienced significant downtime in their operations.

Health risks remain higher in places such as India. Three weeks after the flooding the state government declared an epidemic of leptospirosis in Mumbai and the surrounding area and declared other parts of the region 'hygienically sensitive'. Companies also continue to be concerned about the risk of avian bird flu in south east Asia, which has followed shortly after Sars. In response, many companies prioritise staff health care as a key component of their business contingency plans. One company, for example, noted that it had gone as far as to acquire an ambulance because of the lack of medical resources in the city. Although not traditionally part of their portfolio, many corporate security functions now take responsibility for major health issues, such as pandemics, because of their strategic importance to the company, although they do not tend to cover health and safety at home.

The Centre of Economic Research Group has identified infrastructure funding needs in India of up to $440 billion.[35] Many companies are taking steps to guard against these types of disruptions. For instance, Bangalore frequently experiences blackouts, but many companies there have their own generators to minimise the risk of downtime.[36] One security practitioner explained that when they were setting up their offshore operation in Mumbai they were offered the choice of one of two information pipelines moving information between the UK and India, one through the Mediterranean the other via South Africa. They decided to take both at an increased cost to the company (which was not challenged), and the decision was vindicated soon afterwards when the pipeline going through the Mediterranean was accidentally cut, with no effect on the company's operations.

Reputation

Politicians and unions in the UK and the USA have been quick to react to the growth in offshoring, concerned about public backlash about the movement of jobs to places like India. Against this backdrop, companies must manage the related reputational risks, with corporate security departments having an important role to play. Offshore 'pioneers' had good cause to be concerned about their association with a trend unpopular with their customers, especially those companies relocating 'customer-facing' operations such as call centres. The sense of uneasiness among customers means that companies must work even harder to uphold the highest levels of service. A recent KPMG survey in the UK found that many customers said they were concerned about the increasing trend for banks to set up call centres and processing operations in offshore locations. Over two-thirds of respondents (67 per cent) said they would be very concerned if they knew that their personal banking details were held in a customer service centre outside the UK.[37]

Offshoring provides an excellent example of the new type of cross-organisational, business development role that the corporate security function can play if properly aligned and involved at the strategic as well as tactical level. With the right type of organisational reach and leverage, security can influence the process and help the company to take risks in new markets in a safe and sustainable way. Our research suggests that the corporate security function must take a broad view of its role, incorporating business continuity, reputation management and human resources alongside its traditional lead on security and political risk, and must fight for a seat at the planning, as well as implementation, table.

6. The art of managing up, down and across

The new global business environment is changing the way that companies organise themselves. Most multinational companies have what is termed a 'matrix' structure, where work is arranged around products or projects, rather than hierarchical functions. This allows them to be responsive to markets and better able to deal with external shocks. Our research shows that the corporate security departments that can adopt the same working practices will be well aligned with the business. In a recent academic study, corporate security managers concluded that organisational influences, such as structure, communications, reach, process and internal conflict, have the largest impact on the way they work,[38] but how they affect security, and what the department can do to influence internal dynamics has received relatively little attention.

On the one hand, matrix structures present steep challenges for corporate security because it must work across teams to permeate all areas of the business. On the other hand, its rejection of siloed working makes this structure – when managed correctly – the most conducive to 'commitment-based security' and alignment. Within a matrix structure business functions must manage up, down and across simultaneously and will do this most effectively through trusted relationships, visibility and an understanding of change management.

The rise of the matrix structure

The oldest and probably most well-known structure is the functional structure, where a company is organised around functions, such as finance, marketing, sales and security. While this provides greater clarity of role for employees and produces functional economies of scale, its inflexibility can become problematic as businesses grow and diversify. Its rigid hierarchy can hinder communication between branches, causing unnecessary delays in output or planning. If workers do not see or speak to one another often, companies fail to spot changing customer needs, and become unresponsive to the market. IBM had a functional structure with a strict distinction between functional areas such as marketing and finance. It was believed that this structure led to delays of up to two years in the introduction of new models and this caused IBM's profits to fall. IBM has now split its business into divisions, with each division responsible for one product.[39] As a result, functional structures are best suited to businesses that produce only one product or a closely related group of products.

Most large companies have shifted to a matrix structure, where teams relate to products or projects and bring together a combination of skills, all driven by shared business goals. As might be expected, difficulties can arise around funding allocation and budgeting, and there may also be some duplication of effort, as marketers in one division may not be aware of marketing being done elsewhere.

What marks matrix structures apart from ad hoc project management practices is the presence of a project coordinator, which combines the standard vertical hierarchical structure with a super-imposed lateral or horizontal structure of a project coordinator.[40] These individuals are critical because they act as a conduit for the messages and plans of the specialists into each vertical or functional group. Most companies we spoke to have created a 'group corporate security' function to maintain a strategic outlook on security activity across the business units, coordinate this work, and spread good practice from one part of the company to another. Most also have some form of structure in place – some more formal than others – to provide 'contact points' within the different business units and locations.

The flattened hierarchy eases communication across team or divisional boundaries, increasing visibility and effectiveness. Matrix structures are conducive to localised ideas development rather than diktats from the top. When effectively decentralised, each individual is actively involved in the planning and execution of security measures. Supervisors and managers still have an important role to play, and it is vital that the link between security experts and management remains clear. The security specialists cannot work as a separate entity within the structure; in other words, they cannot be a functional division within a matrix structure.

Effective management within matrix structures

There are a number of theories about effective management in matrix structures. Drawing on various authors,[41] there are three features most relevant to the management of corporate security.

Clear sense of place and function

It is vital that people understand the rationale behind the structure, why working within such complexity will help them to meet their own objectives. It is important to document the relationships between the different axes of the matrix through protocols, contracts or service level agreements, to help people to visualise their own place relative to that of others. They also need to feel they 'belong' to one dimension of the matrix. This will generally be the axis that will support their career aspirations, reflecting professional specialism, limits to personal geographic mobility, personality or skill set. The bonds may be somewhat looser than in a traditional structure, but they nevertheless should be intact in order for people to feel part of a community of sorts, and thus more motivated.

Clear reporting lines

Ambiguities will persist about position, responsibilities and loyalties and they should not be 'managed away'. Companies should, though, ensure they identify and distinguish between an individual's 'firm' and 'dotted' line reporting relationships. This benefits both the manager and the managed, and should extend to clarity about where pay and conditions responsibilities lie, which may be different from the day-to-day 'solid' line reports and professional leadership. Where staff have dual reporting responsibilities they should be protected from potential cross-fire through the creation of a culture within which it is acceptable to escalate a dispute to the directors of the function, profit centres and country or regional units.

Strong relationships

It is imperative to foster close communication and understanding between specialist managers on the different axes, which is likely to involve extensive networking between senior management. Encouraging workers to move across functional areas will also enhance the cross-cutting nature of the structure by increasing their understanding of how the business works, and spreading ideas and best practice.

7. Managing up

Good corporate security management starts at the top of the company; if the board does not 'own' security, understand its relevance to the business and trust the leadership and judgement of the head of security and the security team, alignment will be impossible. Effective upward management is not just about having a close relationship with the CEO or other board members. Corporate security departments need to have comprehensive strategies in place to help them to reach a senior level within their company, have good and frequent contact with the board, have increased senior management understanding of security, and align their work with the business. In the leading companies, security has backing right from the top. The corporate security department must guard against placing too much emphasis on the top at the expense of relationships across and down the business, as will be discussed in later chapters.

Relative seniority

The length of the reporting line between the head of group security and the board has an important influence on the ability of the corporate security function to align itself with the business. Heads of group security we surveyed report directly to the board or are just one or two steps removed from it. One commented: 'The secret of success is to have a short chain of command.' As our survey indicates, 75 per cent of heads of security are one or two steps away from the board. In most cases, heads of security are able to get straight to the top in just one move in the event of operational necessity, regardless of their official reporting structure, although this can be vulnerable to the discretion of one's boss. One of the companies we spoke to is currently trying to formalise this 'dotted' relationship for precisely this reason.

Proximity to the board allows the corporate security function to leverage influence across the company and shortcut decision-making processes, which can be slow in matrix organisations. One former head of security for a major bank reflected on the fact that his lack of seniority had hampered his ability to influence. The group and the business heads had wanted to make a senior appointment but in the end didn't appoint the head of security at a senior enough level. This impacted on the function's ability to operate at the senior management level and affected how others perceived its standing and importance. He reflected: 'At the time I didn't push for level 8 status because my focus was less on promotion and more on building the relationship of the function to the rest of the business, both upwards with the board and across with other related areas of risk. I thought that influence would follow from this, but it didn't.'

The debate continues to rage about whether security should be a board-level position. One head of group security at board level in the UK that we spoke to commented that his seniority helps to establish security as a strategic priority for the company. Others argue that, while security needs to be represented at board level, it does not necessarily have to live there. One said: 'I don't believe that chief security officers have to be on the board; that is a false concept. They need to stand alongside the board and be in board meetings from time to time just as other functions do. You don't need a board member with a security background but someone with responsibility for my portfolio and objectives. Then the head of security needs to flesh out the detail. It certainly helps if there is someone on the board with an interest in security though.'

Level and nature of contact with the board

It is vital that corporate security departments are proactive in communicating and building strong relationships with members of the senior management team. One head of security said: 'I like senior people to know a lot about what we are doing because it helps in getting their support.' Some 30 per cent meet with someone from their board at least once a week, and all present to the board, either formally once or twice per year or when called on to brief on a particular topic, as many have recently with avian flu, for example. For many heads of security, the strength of their relationship with the board is enhanced by the fact that they manage the personal security of board members and their families, which allows them to develop deep and trusted relationships.

This contact is about much more than just having face time with senior management. Heads of security must understand the interests of the board, be happy operating at the highest level, be able to present in a credible way to board members, and value board level input. One commented: 'We need to communicate and present in a way that is consistent with what they expect from all functions at that level. Some heads of security have got to learn that when you are operating at this level you have to be presentation-driven rather than content driven.' Many said they had had to remove someone from a regional post because they were unable to communicate or engage at the highest level: 'I felt we were missing out by not having this exposure, support and credibility.'

Understanding of security by the board

Our research shows that there is very little understanding at board level of the role of corporate security. When we asked heads of security what they thought the expectations of senior management had been when they first assumed their post, responses such as this were typical: 'When I arrived they had no idea what security should or could do. One senior manager told me, "I don't know what you do, I maybe don't want to know what you do, but I know that we need you."'

For effective operators this offers an exciting opportunity to shape the role in the way they want. One described how he has dramatically increased the portfolio of the department, and in doing so enhanced its profile and standing across the company:

> *Security is now seen as being integral; I sit on the senior management team and am a member of the group operational risk committee. When I arrived the company was doing very little about fraud, money laundering and privacy, and we were doing information security but not understanding it as information risk. There was no central focus. The empire building that I have done has created a portfolio and raised awareness of the issues.*

Senior level buy-in is critical. Research carried out by The Conference Board shows that the extent to which the chief executive is convinced of the business case for security has an impact on how corporate security operates.[42] Among the companies surveyed whose chief executives believe security adds business value, two-thirds have increased security spending since 9/11, while 61 per cent of the companies whose executives view security as an expense reported no increase in spending. Their research also showed an impact on access to the board. In companies run by executives who believe in the business case, 32 per cent meet with their security directors once a week or more, and another 32 per cent at least once per month. On the other hand, in companies where the chief executive views security as an expense to be minimised, half of the security directors had not met with the chief executive in the previous 12 months. Direct access goes on to have an impact on security spending. Three-quarters of the companies with weekly security meetings with their senior management reported an increase in security spending after 9/11, compared with only 30 per cent of the companies where the security director and chief executive never met.[43]

The leading corporate security departments invest a lot of time in communicating with the board, which should mean that their successors do not have to start from scratch: 'I have worked hard to move from a situation where the senior management team know about five per cent of what we do to one where they know about 95 per cent of our work. I talk to people about what we do because I want to dispel the "security myth".'

Strategic alignment between security and the business

The most respected heads of security have a clear sense of their own identity, which is about business first, security second: 'I am a business man who happens to have security expertise.' Everyone we interviewed appreciated the economic imperative of the private sector, where 'there is no place for security purists'. One said: 'It is easy to build security that will put a company out of business. We need to apply security with an understanding of the business. Because we work this way, the company rarely takes major decisions without corporate security being involved.' The sense that these corporate security departments are in tune with the business was reinforced when we asked them to tell us about requests for money or resources that have been turned down. One said: 'I don't have an example – you never ask for something you know you won't get. Sometimes we need to reposition something in a more acceptable format. But if you are asking for things and not getting them it's probably because you don't understand the business and the main players well enough.'

What does this actually mean in practice? It is difficult to tell whether this is style rather than substance, or even just rhetoric. Very few of those interviewed were able to confirm their company's current business priorities, beyond the usual business imperatives, such as shareholder value, profit, expansion and reputation management. In structural terms there was little evidence of practices to reinforce strategic alignment between security and the business. For example, very few of the heads of security we spoke to produce a strategic plan showing the aims and objectives of the department against those of the company overall. Only one gave an example of measuring the function directly against business priorities. It has developed a cost–benefit analysis tool that allows it to catalogue security spend against the value generated from it. In some areas of security this is easier to do than others. It is more straightforward and meaningful, for example, to show seizures of illegal products against the total money spent on seizures. It is less easy to measure the intangibles, such as reputation management. In response to the study one board member commented: 'The function is critical to our ability to operate in many markets and gives confidence and reassurance in all.'[44]

One interesting approach to measuring security has been attempted by Bruce Larson, security director at American Water. In a recent article for *CSO Online* Larson suggested that 'value protection is one attempt to overcome security's classic problem of seeming like nothing but a drain on the business'.[45] If the main aims of the business are to increase revenue for the company and/or increase efficiency then security must find another approach that highlights its value. Larson's 'value protection' metric is a ratio that looks like this:

$$VP = (N - E) / N$$

where VP = value protection
       N = normal operations cost ($)
       E = event impact ($)

Steve Schmitt, American Water's vice president of operations, believes that the value protection metric is a response to senior executives wanting 'something that proves the value of security', rather than 'creating reasonable security', and as he points out: 'It's getting us better visibility from the business owners and partners on risks and better ways to mitigate the risks.'[46]

Our research shows that successful heads of security use their position on key committees and working groups to enhance their standing and influence within the company. There is no model that can be replicated; the security function will need to decide which committees to join based on their sector and the internal structure of the company. For example, many heads of security in the financial services sector seek access to the group audit committee because it is one of the most influential groupings for that type of company.

An energy company we spoke to had created a security risk council to drive through minimum standards because there was no such structure in place. The council, whose decisions are endorsed by the board and are a requirement for the UK business, has very senior membership. It includes the general counsel, head of internal audit, the information security manager, the senior human resources manager, all the security risk managers from the five UK businesses along with their managers. This kind of interface is key: 'It's all about connectivity and getting a seat at the table. We have done work identifying networks and partnership opportunities. If there is a committee that controls or influences something we are working on security should have a seat.'

In some cases, these committees can mandate businesses and regions to adopt security measures or standards. In companies where business units value their autonomy, though, mandating should be avoided. For example, one head of security commented: 'One of the ways that we get the businesses on side is by very visibly co-owning their risks. In other words, we approach them with the assumption that we are all in this together. They respond much more positively to that than the big stick approach. That's the worst way to try to change behaviour and practices.'

Others adopt a more informal approach to alignment. Many mentioned the value of feedback: 'We are looking for agreement and enthusiasm from the business, and assurance that what we are doing actively assists them and adds value to the business. In a recent senior level meeting where corporate security was discussed, there was consensus that we don't waste people's time and we add value. That was good enough feedback for me.' A number of other indicators were mentioned: the size of annual bonus, formal feedback solicited at the end of a piece of work, letters of appreciation, requests for more work, and being perceived as being a member of the project team rather than someone from group headquarters who has been brought in as a consultant.

8. Managing down

Within a matrix structure corporate security must not try to act as a distinct function; it must work through business units and regions, transfer responsibility to the local level and influence rather than dictate how others will work. It is still important, though, for it to achieve functional coherence to ensure the company has a common approach to security which is underpinned by a structure that reflects the philosophy.

A clear philosophy for security

The leading heads of security have a clear philosophy for security; they see themselves less as the 'protectors' of the company, and more as the 'function' that enables it to take risks. One said: 'There is no point trying to make us the most secure company in the world; we need to be the most successful company.' Strong leadership is critical to achieving functional coherence, setting the tone for how security is managed throughout the company. When we visited our partners in India and South Africa these messages were repeated right down the chain to the level of local security manager.

Leading, managing and doing require three different skills sets and are rarely done effectively together. It is important that the head of security resists the temptation to get dragged into the detail of delivery, but instead focuses on operating at the strategic level. As one said: 'The role of our department is to look at the group as a whole, at the strategic rather than the tactical level. People within the business do the tactical stuff. Our people at group level should be looking at where the next threat is coming from and how that relates to the business.' This message must be reinforced from the top to ensure the group security team understands its role and place within the structure.

The presence of a group security structure provides an interface with the project coordination role, which is critical in matrix structures. Some companies admitted that they had contemplated whether they still needed group-level capacity at all, but had always come out in favour. One head of security reflected: 'When security was delivered through line management it didn't work; it was more hit and miss and there wasn't the consistency we have now.' The group function is also able to provide resources for regional managers. One security manager in India said that he relied on it to bring him up to speed with security issues across the globe and across the group, and to expand networks. Similarly, a security manager in South Africa said: 'The support we get from Group is critical. They build relationships with my superiors which really helps, and we regularly exchange ideas.'

Business and regional integration

Companies have a variety of structural approaches to achieving business and regional integration, but all of the leading businesses share a commitment to integration, regardless of the detail of their model. Some security managers report through the function and have dotted-line reporting through the businesses and the regions. Conversely, others devolve as much reporting as possible to the business or region, maintaining only a small group security capacity. Most have a regional security layer to bridge the gap between group and individual business operating units. For some companies the firm and dotted reporting lines are clearly and formally defined, while others have adopted a more flexible approach.

Within the constraints of this research project, it is not possible to draw detailed conclusions about which models are best suited to particular sectors or areas of the world. We can, though, make a number of observations which might help companies to think about how they structure their corporate security function to ensure it is integrated at the business and regional level.

Most companies have a regional security layer, which acts as a conduit between the group and business units. It also has specialist knowledge of the region, can spot trends across a number of countries, and act as a local fixer. It can be one of the most difficult positions to get right, though, and is to a large extent dependent on relationships with local business executives. One European regional head of security for an American company stressed the importance of business or regional reporting: 'If I had a dotted line to someone senior in Europe, I would be able to get top level feedback on what was really concerning the company and local feedback from my peers about my performance. It would also be useful to have someone here in Europe who could open doors for me in my region.'

Regional security managers run the risk of overstretch. They tend to spend a lot of time travelling and find themselves having similar discussions with each of their businesses and country units. To overcome this, one company we met in South Africa has established 'cluster security managers' to mirror their newly established 'cluster business leader' model. Each cluster security manager deals with the security needs of all the businesses within their cluster, similar to the country manager role, and sits in on business, country and regional planning meetings to ensure integration and ease the workload.

For companies with a smaller global footprint the regional security model might not be necessary. Most companies we spoke to are very large multinationals, with operations on just about every continent. One of the companies, though, operates only in Europe, Asia and the USA. It was the only company without regional coordination, and the head of security argues that an extra layer is unnecessary. Its group security department is staffed by functional specialists who link directly to named contacts within each of the businesses.

Responsibility for security is delegated to the business operating unit, which means that the role of the group security department is to influence rather than dictate. One head of security commented: 'Because of the autonomous nature of the operating business mandating security is not an option. Ours is very much a role of persuading the businesses that what you want to do makes sense to them and will help them to meet their business aims.' Because of this, most local security managers tend to report into the business rather than through the function. Sometimes they have a dedicated security manager, but more often than not it is someone with a wider portfolio. One head said: 'We have people regionally with "security" in their job description but not in their title. They are genuinely part of the business. That's how my company wants it.' The exact configuration of their role depends on the nature and extent of risks faced, the corporate culture and historical precedent.

Clarity within a matrix organisation is key, but so is flexibility, which means that lines should not become too rigid. Being able to manage in different directions and work outside one's brief to get the job done is important within complex matrix structures, and corporate security must find ways of working allow it to do that. In the face of complexity, most people tend to try to simplify reality to make it easier to understand and manage. This might be comforting, but ultimately it is the organisations that are able to embrace complexity and 'mess' that will win in the long term.[47] One head of security said: 'In the security world, I like fuzzy edges and overlaps. Clear delineations can allow things to drop through the gaps.'

Budgets

A number of companies noted that budgetary arrangements have a big impact on their ability to influence decision-making at the local level. Most of the leading corporate security departments have a relatively small central budget for group corporate security, which covers the costs of the central administration and travel. In the normal course of providing advice, guidance and policy, the group department does not have to ask for money from the businesses or regions. As one regional head of security said: 'Having to talk about money would stop doors opening.'

There is then a split between those who bill directly for work they do for a particular business, and those whose additional budget is paid for collectively by all parts of the company according to a set formula for the division of costs. This basic model is most effective at achieving alignment because security is forced to operate in ways that add value to the business. One head of security reflected: 'Security does not have a God-given right. We have to market our services and help others to see the value we can bring to them.'

There is no evidence to suggest that this model stops corporate security departments doing what they think is necessary. None of the leading heads of security we spoke to were able to provide an example of a time when they had asked for money and been refused. One said: 'If you understand the company and what it needs properly you should always pitch your ideas in a way that will be justifiable to the business. If not, you are almost certainly asking for something you don't need.' This could of course mean that they are compromising on what they feel they need rather than being highly influential, but this was dismissed. One said: 'I am confident that I can either authorise or get support for about 99 per cent of what we want to do. Sometimes we need to reposition something in a more acceptable format. For example, we sometimes have problems in getting people to understand information assurance because it's not widely known about or accepted. But this is beginning to change and will change.'

For most, this position has been earned rather than inherited. Many reflected that they hadn't always been able to get what they wanted. One said: 'Previously, the security budget was very small and I had to fight to get increases. But I don't need to work like that any more.' A former head of security who was the first person in the role and therefore had to establish the function commented: 'We walked a difficult tight rope between being responsible for security but having no resource or authority to actually do it. We were trying to galvanise the response and give advice, but couldn't actually DO very much.'

The leading heads of security recognise that to be successful they need to work through organisational structures that reflect both their philosophy for security and the organisational culture of their company. Most have worked hard to shape these structures to deliver maximum benefit for them through influence and reach down through the business.

9. Managing across

Managing across a matrix organisation is made easier when companies have established the necessary structures, processes and cultures for managing up and down. Corporate security departments also require good social networks, high levels of awareness of the function and effective approaches to change management to be truly effective. These are aspects of the role that were emphasised strongly during interviews and discussions, but which tend to be overlooked by most of the literature. They are perhaps the most important factors influencing the ability of the function to align itself with the business, change the way the company thinks about security, and shift behaviour right across the company.

Trusted social networks

We have focused so far on the formal structure and networks within companies, but the changing nature of the corporate environment, especially the new prevalence of matrix organisations, means that most work within organisations now gets done through networks of employees rather than fixed teams. These networks do not appear on formal organograms, but are intricately intertwined with an organisation's performance, the way it develops and executes strategy, and its ability to innovate. For most people, networks have an important impact on personal productivity, learning and career success. A study by the Institute for Strategic Change showed that high performers are not distinguished by their individual expertise, but by the size and diversity of their personal networks.[48] One head of security commented: 'Getting things done is all about building close personal relationships with people. We are constantly building relationships, working hard with all parts of the business, across all departments.'

A study into social networks in the work place by Rob Cross and Andrew Parker came to three conclusions,[49] which have important implications for current assumptions about how corporate security is managed and aligned with the business.

1   *Mid-level mangers tend to emerge as being key to effective information flows.* Currently, heads of security place a great deal of emphasis on the quality of their relationship with senior executives, which is understandable given the growing maturity of the function. One head of security said: 'Our middle managers, especially, still don't know what we do.' When asked to identify the key points for collaboration within the company none of the interviewees mentioned middle management. The function needs to reach out more to middle management.

2   *Senior people are often too removed from the day-to-day running of things.* Again, this underlines the need for the security function to place more emphasis on their relationships further down the chain.

3   *Physical separation prevents serendipitous meetings that are so important to network formation.* Anecdotally, many lament the amount of travel they and their team have to do. They instinctively understand the need for face time, but there is a danger of overstretch if the group security function tries to do too much. This suggests that a layered approach might be more effective and relieve some of the pressure on group security.

Building the type of trusted relationships that are found within social networks challenges security professionals to think about and present themselves differently. Too often, they assume that their value to the company comes through their content knowledge. This is of course important in establishing credibility and authority, but is not their only source of authority.

A study by the Institute for Knowledge-Based Organizations found that there are two types of trust. First, competence-based trust, which focuses on ability. People do not need to have high levels of trust to seek out surface-level information from experts. Second, and particularly important for security within matrix organisations, is benevolence-based trust, which is related to vulnerability.[50] It requires us to expose our lack of knowledge and ask the questions we need answered. When people have this kind of trust they are more likely to be creative, learning what they need to so they can do something better or differently. This is critical if individuals across the company are to play an active role in delivering security, rather than leaving it to the corporate security department.

This relates directly to the way in which the corporate security function builds relationships across the business. It should be taken as given that the security function needs the functional expertise to be able to perform its job, and this will build competence-based trust as a result. Benevolence-based trust is more important in aligning security with the business though. It is the type of trust that encourages a business to seek out the corporate security department for help, particularly relating to a sensitive issue, where it has a problem, or where it has made a mistake which needs to be resolved. Only if the relationship is founded on benevolence-based trust will it have confidence that problems will be solved in the right manner, with discretion, and that it will be met with understanding rather than judgement by the corporate security department.

Cross and Parker's study identified ten actions for promoting interpersonal trust, which chime with our research: act with discretion; match words and deeds; communicate often and well; establish a shared vision and language; highlight knowledge domain boundaries; know when to step out of your role; give away something of value; help people refine unclear ideas; make decisions fair and transparent; and hold people accountable for trustworthy behaviour.

Raising awareness of security

Security does not have a mandate and must 'sell' its services to the rest of the company. Studies show that there are two key factors influencing the likelihood of a person being sought out for information or help. First, they must know and value what you do. Regardless of organisational structure, people won't connect with new projects if they are unaware of others' skills and expertise. Second, they must be able to get timely access to you.[51]

The leading corporate security departments invest a lot of time and energy to raise visibility and understanding of their work across the company, including some of the following activities:

General

- O security presentations and training within staff induction courses
- O regular presentations on security, both for specially convened groups, as well as slots within other people's meetings
- O regular emails about particular aspects of security, or in response to an incident or staff concerns
- O articles for the company newsletter
- O security page on the company intranet portal
- O regular security awareness surveys, which not only provide useful information about the nature and extent of awareness, but help to create visibility themselves, too.

Services for staff

- O personal and travel safety presentations, either specially organised, or to take place in locations where staff will be anyway, such as lunch halls
- O easy-to-read booklets on various aspects of security – one company had distributed these to the homes of all employees

○ plastic credit-card-style card containing emergency phone numbers
○ security department freebies with practical use for staff.

Regionally
○ professionally produced monthly regional newsletter, tailored to the interests and needs of each region
○ fortnightly bulletin on country risk, which acts as a valuable service for the country and region, but also as a 'flag carrier' for security
○ regional conferences to bring together representatives from each of the businesses to discuss a particular issue, such as fraud, kidnapping, terrorism and so forth
○ regional visits from group security
○ presence of a security coordinator in all locations to be the face of security on the ground.

Change management
Charles Darwin said: 'It is not the strongest of the species that survive, nor the most intelligent, but the one most responsive to change.' Similarly, a company's future success depends on its capacity to change in response to its environment or market. If security is to be aligned with the business, it must be effective at change management and be able to embed a security approach across the business, which will evolve over time with the commitment and buy-in of staff. The security strategy must respond not only to security threats, but to the full range of factors influencing global companies and the complexities that are an everyday part of doing business. One head of security said: 'Those who are constantly looking for change will always be closer to the business.'

Most companies have a poor record of change management though. John Kotter estimates that 85 per cent of companies fail to achieve needed transformations. There are a number of theories to explain the lack of take-up. Paul Strebel reports that 50–80 per cent of change efforts in Fortune 1000 companies fail because employees fail to recognise what is driving the change and the value it can bring to them and the business as a whole. Larry Hirshman says the problem is due to the fact that organisational change projects are treated as separate projects rather than as part of the day-to-day running of the business. And William Bridges argues that companies need to recognise that people need time to go through the psychological steps of giving up old ways before embracing new ones. He observes that companies normally invest most of their time, energy and resources in the change project itself, and very little in supporting the people expected to make the change happen in practice.[52]

Andrea Shapiro argues that organisations change only when individuals within them do, which is usually because they are enthusiastic about the idea. She likens the spread of ideas – and changed practices – within companies to the spread of a virus. Three things must be present: content or 'stickiness', the value of the change being suggested; carriers or advocates for change; and context or having the right environmental support and incentives in place to sustain the change. Table 2 shows a comparison between factors

Table 2. Comparison between the factors affecting the spread of flu with those affecting the spread of organisational change

Factors affecting spread of flu	Factors affecting spread of organisational change
Virulence of flu strain	Intrinsic value of the organisational change
Contacts between contagious people	Contacts between advocates and apathetics
Environmental factors, such as levels of sanitation and medical care	Environmental factors, such as bonuses for successful implementation

Source: Shapiro, *Creating Contagious Commitment*

affecting the spread of flu and those affecting the spread of organisational change.[53]

Creating enthusiasm for change is critical for the effectiveness of the security function. This requires the function to open up its work and thinking to the rest of the company. For too long, secrecy has seemed an important factor in building the credibility and authority of the department. But in today's multinational companies it is a straitjacket rather than a safety blanket, which must be abandoned if alignment is to be achieved. As long as security remains a 'dark art' the function will never make its mark on the company.

10. Skills for corporate security

For many years corporate security has been dominated by a 'defensive' approach, focused on protection and loss prevention. The head of security was seen as little more than the 'guard at the gate', someone whose actions invariably stopped people doing their jobs instead of enabling the business to function more effectively. Typically, heads of security came from a narrow talent pool, namely police, armed forces or intelligence. Martin Broughton, Chairman of BA, described the old approach to corporate security thus: 'The old corporate cop who applied the skills of his former life, much as he would have done before, yet without a measured understanding of the new context.'[54]

The Conference Board survey confirmed that the corporate security field in the USA is still predominantly staffed by ex-police and servicemen.[55] Of those surveyed, almost three-quarters came from a traditional security background: 31 per cent from police, 19 per cent from intelligence and 21 per cent from the armed forces (see figure 1). Furthermore, there are almost no women or people from minority ethnic groups in this role.

There are many understandable reasons why companies tend to recruit security managers from these backgrounds. The police and armed forces churn out individuals with intensive training in the practice of security and protection, and have a wealth of hands-on experience that is scarcely available elsewhere. In the absence of any formal or recognised qualification for security management, and

Figure 1. Professional backgrounds of security managers

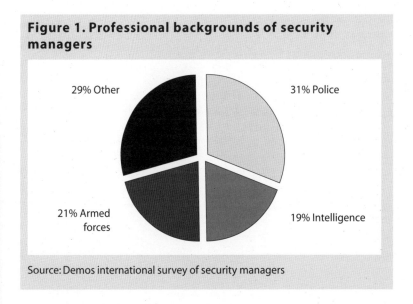

29% Other

31% Police

21% Armed forces

19% Intelligence

Source: Demos international survey of security managers

given the paucity of knowledge about corporate security within most boardrooms, this is a pretty logical form of quality control for companies to adopt.

Our research points to a new vision for corporate security which is led at a strategic rather than tactical level to reflect its importance to the company (the top end for a head of group security in Europe is now approximately £150,000, with variable bonuses of 25–40 per cent[56]), which is delivered through a much more dynamic security team. Still the exception rather than the rule, though, there are signs in the companies we spoke to that some senior management teams are beginning to ask for more diversity. One head of security commented: 'In the past, we have tended to recruit people with 100 per cent security skills and then had the difficult challenge of teaching these people business skills. We now appreciate the need to bring together mixed and varied teams.' This reflects our own research which showed that only 22 per cent of heads of security we surveyed had some form of business experience before assuming their current role. Evidence suggests that developments in this area are far less advanced than in others, and there is still much work to do before the security team of the future becomes a reality.

The case for change

There are a number of reasons why greater diversity is essential within the corporate security function.

First, there is a growing recognition of the strategic importance of security and as a result security departments need to operate at a much more senior level. This requires a whole new skills set, which privileges leadership, communication, presentation and networking above content or tactical knowledge. The divide between strategic and tactical thinkers is one of the important distinguishing factors for companies that have effectively aligned their business with security, and those individuals who are unable to make this leap will continuously hit a self-imposed glass ceiling and will struggle to achieve the type of influence and leverage that many of those we spoke to have attained.

Second, matrix organisations require a particular approach to management and leadership, which can be antithetical to those with police or armed services backgrounds. These types of institutions tend towards command and control management styles where there is a relatively high degree of certainty that orders issued at the top of an organisation will be delivered right the way down. In today's corporate environment, the impact of the security department is proportionate to its ability to persuade individuals and teams all over the company to collaborate and cooperate. This means that dialogue between security specialists and non-specialists is essential.[57] It also makes it more important that the security function is representative of its 'customer base'. If it cannot speak to, understand and relate to the full range of employees – men, women, young, old, different nationalities, faiths and ethnicities – it will find it more difficult to achieve genuine integration and alignment.

Third, traditional security skills are associated with an approach where security is perceived as a 'dis-enabler' of business. Those with formal security training can tend to be risk averse, while businesses need to take calculated risks to stay ahead of competitors, break into new markets and maximise profits. A recruitment consultant commented: 'Chief executives don't want a security manager who constantly tells them what they can't do. They want people who will help them to push the boundaries without unduly compromising the company.' This means they need people who understand the realities of doing business and who are not security purists. One head of security observed: 'You need to feel comfortable operating the 80/20 rule – 80 per cent is usually good enough. You can always go back later to fix the other 20 per cent if you need to. The ability to compromise is key; people who like controlled organisations will struggle.'

Fourth, the corporate security function needs people who are happy breaking rules, innovating and thinking outside the box.[58] Studies of security-related professions such as the police, the ambulance service and local authority emergency planning departments have suggested that 'too much' experience in a traditional security context can inhibit people from making innovative responses to security incidents. Heads of security consistently rated qualities such as independent thinking, willingness to challenge assumptions and behaviours and innovation as being ones they value most in their team. One said: 'I'm looking for people who push the boundaries and constantly challenge the way we work.'

Fifth, there is a growing recognition of the value of 'the human element'. According to experts, many security professionals are typically trained to address security incidents and emergencies in ways that fail to factor in the human dynamics of such situations, including the impact of emotions, perceptions and fear on people's behaviour. Emotional intelligence is critical to effective alignment, but the human element of security and risk management is routinely overshadowed by the emphasis on technical security skills.

Professor Edward Borodzicz has argued that security and risk specialists need to have a grasp of how risk is socially constructed (among non-specialists) in non-rational ways and respond in ways that are sensitive to the concerns and fears of staff, regardless of whether or not they are logical. That is not to say that companies should waste money on pointless measures, but at times of heightened anxiety they must appreciate that the emotional wellbeing of employees is just as important as their physical safety.[59]

Business skills

For security to be aligned with the business, security managers must understand the business and how they contribute towards its objectives. Only 22 per cent of the security managers we surveyed had prior business experience before moving into corporate security, and only a handful have an MBA. There is evidence that business skills are becoming more important to companies; one specialist recruitment consultant observed that his clients are increasingly requesting candidates who have *not* had a long first career in the police or armed forces because they want to avoid candidates encumbered by the kind of experience that encourages a 'boxed' way of thinking about security. The excerpts from two sample executive search assignments from SSR Personnel highlight the growing importance of business skills at the higher end of security management.[60]

Chief security officer – Worldwide retailer
Salary £125,000
Reporting to: As a plc board member, the candidate has significant empowerment and budget-holding with subsidising business units.
Location: Central Europe
Professional qualifications: Educated to business degree or equiva-lent; professional membership; to have experience of corporate associations, such as International Security Management Association (ISMA) would be preferred; professional qualifications such as Certified Protection Professional would be an advantage.
Experience: A senior manager with commercial experience; sound practical understanding of the operation of a large corporate head

office essential and knowledge of the retail industry an advantage; must have planning ability together with budgetary control skills and experience of managing people in a multinational environment.

Personal characteristics: An outgoing personality with well-developed interpersonal skills, capable of relating to people at every level; a competent oral and written presenter who can think logically and progressively, especially when under pressure.

Director of security – Insurance group

Salary £95,000

Knowledge (ratio)

Technical (30%): Knowledge of security practices and principles in an international environment; managerial experience with multinational responsibility for physical, operational, technical and information security, contingency planning, investigations and security awareness programmes.

Business (20%): Good analytical skills; strategic outlook; exposure to financial services, banking or similar business environments.

Managerial (30%): Ability to handle multiple tasks simultaneously; willingness to manage or to personally execute necessary tasks, as limited resources require.

Interpersonal (20%): Cross-cultural sensitivity; good motivational skills, effective at leadership through consultation and influence; outstanding written and oral communication skills.

A number of companies have adopted this model. Security is a seconded position at one of the large oil companies, occupied by a different person every two years. Their current head of security is a woman from a marketing background. Another extractive company has an engineer as head of security. One large British company has recently appointed a new head of security who, although he has seven years of military experience, was recruited specifically because of his senior business experience. All his predecessors had traditional security backgrounds, but the company wanted a very different type of person: 'Other parts of the business had modernised, but not security. They wanted someone who was connected to the business already, someone who had consumed the services of security and appreciated the importance of security through the eyes of our customers. They did want the reassurance that my short stint in the army was able to provide, but that was not the overriding factor.' He does not see his relative lack of security experience as an inhibitor: 'I haven't come across any problems relating to this yet. My advantage is that I really understand the business.'

Even those with a traditional security profile talk more about the value of their business acumen than their security-specific skills. One with both security and business experience said: 'I draw most heavily on my business experience.' A former intelligence officer with no business experience referred to the benefits of his experience, but with reference solely to generic management experience: 'It has provided me with specific skills that are needed for this job: handling senior people, clear and effective communication, managing large teams, being clear about priorities and delegating things that are less important, assessing risk, and being confident about making judgements in front of senior management. My skills provide a good fit at this level but not further down the chain. I don't know the detail of how things need to be done, but that isn't a problem in this role.'

There is growing evidence that security experience may not be necessary, or even desirable, for heads of security. But surely it is critical further down the chain, when real security problems have to be solved? Again, the picture is unclear. The fact that companies continue to target individuals with specific skills – investigations, analysis, fraud detection and so forth – would tend to suggest that they are needed and valued. However, a good number of the leading companies have a mixture of 'experts' and 'non-experts' within their departments, and some have created teams within their businesses that have no security experience at all. One commented: 'I wanted security to be truly integrated and it was therefore more important for me that my security team understands the business than has an intimate knowledge of three-pin locks. There is a lot of scepticism about our model from peers who can't conceive of a security function without security. But it works for us and results should speak for themselves.' The second company is so keen on the model, which was developed in the UK, that it has decided to roll it out to business operations overseas. Others are developing centres of excellence around specific skills which means that each location does not need to have a full complement of security skills within its team, but can draft them in from elsewhere, as necessary.

The job specification for security risk managers for one of these companies shows the range of business and soft skills that are valued above security experience.

> ### Security risk adviser – Major energy company
> *Key skill requirements:* Proven experience in the management of projects and a track record of pro-activity in delivering change; knowledge and previous involvement in managing risk and risk-reporting processes, including an understanding of the requirements of the Sarbanes-Oxley Act; awareness of the requirements and benefits of effective business continuity planning; a good understanding of the company's business and the security risk it gives rise to; the ability to exercise sound judgement in dealing with security-related and personal safety issues; excellent presentation skills and the ability to influence colleagues and instil confidence throughout the company and at senior management level through a diplomatic approach; good analytical and report writing skills with an emphasis on accuracy and attention to detail; an understanding of the complexity and sensitivity of investigations and a willingness to gain a detailed knowledge of company discipline procedures and current legislation; the ability to manage production relationships with law enforcement personnel and security industry agencies to ensure that the company has access to the best available information and support.

Personal attributes and behaviours: Strategic focus; accuracy and attention to detail; interpersonal skills; communicates to influence; change and project management; customer-focused; self-confident team player; planning and organising; determination to succeed.

Soft skills

There are a number of reasons for the emerging interest in 'soft' or non-technical security skills. First, the long-neglected 'human factor' in security management has finally come to the fore, and new skills are needed to address this. As one commentator argues: 'Many security managers are beginning to realise that the secret of effective corporate security rests less on their technical expertise (though this is clearly still important), and more on their ability to respond to the human complexities.'[61] Second, as we have seen, in today's global security environment, new models of corporate security are gaining credence. Positioning security at the strategic, executive level of companies means that security managers – especially the most senior – require a wider range of competencies, including softer skills. Finally, due to the complexity of today's global business operations, effective security increasingly relies on the cooperation of a wide range of staff across the organisation. This means not only that communicating security at all levels is vital, but also that the skills, knowledge and training of non-security staff may be equally critical to the delivery of security.

David Foote, president of Foote Partners, suggests that companies need 'a variety of soft skills within their corporate security function, including a positive attitude, diplomacy, patience, attention to detail, tenacious abstract problem-solving ability and a strong will . . . employers must scrutinize candidates for how well they work with others, on teams and with customers, as this is important in cutting through resistance and raising security mind share'.[62]

The ASIS International *Chief Security Officer Guideline* expands this profile further, recommending that chief security officers (CSOs) have 'exceptionally strong . . . interpersonal skills . . . a remarkably high degree of emotional maturity and the ability to calmly facilitate the appropriate resolution of difficult ethical and crisis situations', in addition to, 'the ability to analyse, understand, and explain the value proposition of security initiatives'.[63] When we asked heads of security to identify the most important skills and qualities of their team, they mentioned soft skills far more than technical skills:

O communication skills – people who are able to tailor their messages to their audience
O presentation skills – both formal presentation skills, and people who present themselves well and act with authority and credibility
O diplomacy – people who can get on with a wide range of people and persuade them to cooperate
O natural networkers, both within and outside the company – people need to be able to draw on skills, advice and expertise from a wide network
O personal drive and commitment – they valued people who would go the extra mile, are committed to the work and have a passion for results.

Effective leadership for aligning security with the business

He is an awesome individual. He has an amazing ability to influence people's thinking, convincing them that what he's doing is the right thing. He speaks with authority. He is a charismatic leader.

Regional head of security talking about
his group head of security

'Leadership' was cited by all heads of security as a key reason for their own effectiveness. Studies suggest that leaders have a number of qualities or characteristics, only one of which relates to content knowledge:

O   technical or specific skills related to their role

O   initiative and entrepreneurial drive

O   charismatic inspiration – attractiveness to others and the ability to leverage this esteem to motivate others

O   preoccupation with the role – a dedication that consumes much of the leader's life

O   a clear sense of purpose or mission, embodied in focused goals

O   results oriented – someone who directs every action towards a mission and prioritises activities to spend time where results accrue most

O   optimism – very few pessimists become leaders

O   rejection of determinism – a belief in one's ability to 'make a difference'

O   ability to encourage and nurture those who report to them – and delegate in such a way that allows people to grow

O   role models – leaders may adopt a persona that encapsulates their mission and lead by example

O   self-knowledge (in non-bureaucratic structures)

O   self-awareness – the ability to 'lead' (as it were) one's own self prior to leading other selves similarly

O   with regard to people and to projects, the ability to choose winners – recognising that, unlike with skills, one cannot in general teach attitude; picking winners is not achieved through luck; decisions are based on realistic insight

O   understanding what others say, rather than listening to how they say things – 'walking in someone else's shoes'.[64]

There are, of course, a number of different leadership styles, most of which are defined according to the nature of the relationship between the 'leader' and the 'led'. Broadly speaking there are three main styles: democratic (open and participatory), authoritarian (do as I say because I say so) and laissez-faire (get on with it and I will back you all the way). The corporate security department must be led with a democratic style that encourages participation across the company.

The democratic style of leadership is also called the participative style as it encourages employees to be a part of the decision-making. The democratic manager keeps his or her employees informed about everything that affects their work and shares decision-making and problem-solving responsibilities. This style requires the leader to be a coach who has the final say, but gathers information from staff members before making a decision.[65] Democratic leaders quickly appreciate the strong link between education and democracy. All learning influences the potential realities of our environment, and the political environment influences all learning. Therefore, a knowledgeable work force is ready to be empowered and needs empowerment to remain vital.[66]

There are times when this style is inappropriate. It can sometimes be more cost-effective for the manager alone simply to take the decision, which is particularly true if the manager cannot afford mistakes.[67] This situation is most likely to arise either at a time of crisis or critical moment, or when a consensus cannot be reached but a decision is needed. In this scenario, leaders must be able to rely on their credibility and standing within their team and the organisation to avoid further confrontation or displeasure about behaving in this way. There is also an expectation from senior managers that heads of security should 'get on with the job'. Boards do not have time to be consulted about every decision, although they do want to remain engaged at critical times.

Heads of security tend to need to adopt a laissez-faire approach at times to give their staff the space to make decisions on the ground. All those we interviewed rated the ability of their team to work without tight management. Most spoke about their team in glowing terms, recognised that competent people were at the centre of effective security management, and wanted to give them space to develop and grow. This is particularly true for large multinationals that rely on their regional security managers to work without constant reference to the group level. When asked about the benefits of his boss's leadership style, one regional head of security said: 'What's great about him is that he trusts me to get on with my job.' This approach is usually appropriate only when leading a team of highly motivated and skilled people, who have produced excellent work in the past.[68]

Mechanisms for change

Human resources is fast becoming the most important priority for the corporate security function. The majority of the companies we spoke to rated it as one of their top concerns, whether related to succession planning, defining the right skills set for security managers, building business skills or creating deeper structures that allow security managers to grow up through the business and provide deeper talent pools for the head of security to choose from.

Basic development work

Most leading companies have the normal staff development structures and processes in place. As one head of security said: 'Development is very much part of the game.' This includes the usual raft of training courses, mentoring schemes and development programmes. One company, which is putting considerable time and resources into staff development, has initiated a mentoring programme that involves all members of the corporate security function being mentored by two non-security colleagues. This has the double benefit of giving them exposure to the business and raising security awareness outside the function. That company's head of security commented: 'This scheme has increased business contact and understanding, has created security champions of business people, and has meant that the security function is now included in a much broader range of decision-making forums.'

Fast-tracking those with leadership potential

Most companies operate a 'fast-track' list for their high fliers destined for senior management. These people receive additional development opportunities and are rotated around the business to ensure they get exposure to a range of functions and regions. Many of the companies recognise the importance of getting their security people onto this list, but very few have managed to achieve this so far. One major multinational with close to 100 people in its security team – at group level, regionally and locally – has only three people on its company's fast-track list of employees with group-level leadership potential. This is certainly a promising area of growth for the security function as it would help to raise its profile and standing and would act as a major incentive for potential recruits.

Rotation – around the business and geographically

One of the ways in which the security function could build business acumen and raise the profile of the function is through rotation programmes that send its staff to work in other areas of the business and bring people from elsewhere into the security department for short periods of time. Most heads of security we spoke to agreed this would help them to achieve alignment, but none had managed to make it work in practice. One explained that he is keen to implement such a scheme and has secured backing from the European director: 'We haven't rotated anyone, but we have discussed it. The director for Europe sees no reason why we can't do it through, for example, an exchange programme, but we need to develop our thinking much more. We are thinking about offering this as an option for the high flyers within the regions. We could offer them six months at global headquarters to get exposure to global issues or rotate them into other businesses.'

Others have decided against outwards rotation because of the practical difficulties of making it work. Some said it would put too great a strain on the department to lose a member of staff, even if just for a few months. Others worried about the pressure on receiving departments of supporting people without the necessary skills set. One head of security said: 'We haven't tended to send people from here into other parts of the business. This is because the people we have tended to recruit don't have business skills so would need too much support working in another department.' This seems like a vicious circle that needs to be broken.

There is universal enthusiasm within the leading departments about bringing business talent into the security function. One company is looking into the idea of business high flyers spending short periods of time within the security function: 'We are currently having discussions with various group VPs about the possibility of rotating rising business stars into security for a while. They seem to like the idea but we are still working it through.'

There has been much greater success in regional rotation within the security function. Most companies we spoke to mentioned the importance of sending their security staff to work in other parts of the world, especially in multinational companies where international exposure is an essential part of personal development. One head of security said: 'Part of the rationale for our current European head of security moving to Hong Kong is to gain the international experience that you need to be able to get on within this company.'

Priority setting and review

One concrete way of reinforcing business perspectives within the department is through the priority-setting and review process. However, only one company we spoke to was doing this. The head of security said: 'We have tags into all the business segments. Security proposes the objectives and segment checks and we then reach a compromise. We also cross-reference segment objectives against objectives for security staff. At the end-of-year assessment the segment people input into our appraisals and their comments are especially important in determining our bonuses because they report not only on what we have done but also how we have done it.' This is highly unusual, but an interesting model for companies to observe.

Qualifications

There is growing acceptance of the need for recognised programmes of training and accreditation in corporate security, for a clear career development path to offer bright new graduates, and for professional bodies to represent corporate security professionals. One head of security commented: 'There is a growing feeling within our company that if security is going to stand up alongside the other functions we need to develop capabilities and competencies. We need to be in a position where we have the right people with the right skills, or where skills are lacking training to bring them up to the standard.' There is also consensus that the profession has a long way to go. Howard Schmidt, chief information security officer of eBay, has commented that 'the training ground doesn't yet exist'; for executive level corporate security professionals, 'there is no CSO Institute'.[69]

There are a number of efforts under way to plug this gap. In the USA, a new group of security executives, calling themselves the Global CSO Council, aims to provide guidance to both academia and the security profession in shaping the CSO role.[70] This group has been working to determine the ideal CSO skills set and define a framework for certification and training. The ASIS Guidelines similarly have begun to address this need,[71] while in the UK, a new, employer-led, skills and standards setting body for the security business sector, Skills for Security, has recently been set up.[72]

Various academic qualifications in security and risk management are on offer in both the USA and the UK, particularly at the postgraduate level, but course content is far from standardised across institutions. In the USA, the most widely recognised courses are the Wharton/ASIS Program for Security Executives, a two-week certificate course taught by the same faculty who teach Wharton Business School's prestigious MBA programme, and the ISMA Leadership Program at Georgetown University, run in conjunction with Northwestern's Kellogg School of Management. Both these courses are exclusively for senior-level security executives, and offer a grounding in business, leadership and management skills, matching many of the recommendations laid down by ASIS.

In the UK, postgraduate qualifications in security and risk management are offered at Portsmouth and Leicester universities. Professor Edward Borodzicz is currently setting up a new programme at Goldsmiths University, and the Institute of Risk Management (IRM) also runs its own diploma. The range of material covered in the postgraduate syllabuses is diverse and overlaps extensively with areas such as risk, business continuity management and even criminology.

There is widespread consensus about the need for a degree of standardisation and for formal accreditation and training. According to recruitment specialists in the field of corporate security, employers have begun to look for benchmarks of success and achievement, such as academic qualifications, when recruiting candidates for corporate security roles. This is not surprising given that boards are now more interested in security than ever before, but as we have seen, often do not know what they are looking for. Some of this work is being driven forward by bodies such as ASIS, but much of it is happening within and between companies themselves, partly driven by a perceived failure of these external initiatives to meet their specific needs. One head of security commented: 'We are creating a "model security manager" to help in the recruitment process. This would be much better than the generic stuff we get from recruitment consultants. The skills and qualifications available in our field from people like ASIS and The Security Institute just don't measure up.' Similarly, a group of companies under the umbrella of the Risk and Security Management Forum is currently sponsoring research at Cranfield University on useful qualifications for security management.

Given that there are many different layers of security management in today's complex business environment, these need to be accommodated in the process of designing standards and accreditation; a one-size-fits-all approach will not work. As discussed, different skills and experience are required at the strategic and operational levels. At the strategic level, for instance, ASIS has argued that 'strategic, business and interpersonal abilities' are more important than technical security skills.[73] This is supported by our research, which shows that heads of security consider business and leaderships skills far more important than their security content knowledge.

In institutionalising standards, there is a potential risk that a 'universalist' approach to corporate security will be adopted, or a single career path promoted over and above others. It is important that security and risk management courses cover a range of material and reflect the diversity of skills, experience and approaches to training which add value to the sector. The practice of security is also highly context-specific, which means it cannot be standardised easily. One potential way of avoiding this is to develop a modular approach, based on a basic standard of security training for corporate security professionals, complemented by one or more areas of specialist, technical knowledge and other management and communication skills. Alternatively, others have argued that corporate security should become a common component on MBA courses.

11. Conclusion

In the last five years security has risen up the corporate agenda and in some companies it enjoys relative seniority and influence. Learning from the 'secrets of success' of the leading companies and the shortcomings of others, this report presents a vision of twenty-first-century corporate security that meets the challenges of twenty-first-century companies. The function must take its lead from business drivers rather than specific threats and ensure that the way it works, what it does and how it behaves reflect the new realities of doing business in a complex and fast-moving world.

There are six characteristics of alignment between security and the business:

1 The principle role of the security department is to convince colleagues across the business to deliver security through their everyday actions and decisions – not try to do security to or for the company.
2 The security department is in the business of change management rather than enforcement and works through trusted social networks of influence.
3 Security is there to help the company to take risks rather than prevent them and should therefore be at the forefront of new business development.
4 Security constantly responds to new business concerns

· and, as such, the portfolio of responsibilities and their relative importance will change over time. Security departments should never stand still or become fixed entities. In many companies today, its role is more concerned with overall corporate resilience than 'traditional' security.

5   Security is both a strategic and operational activity, and departments must distinguish between these two layers.

6   The power and legitimacy of the security department does not come from its expert knowledge, but from its business acumen, people skills, management ability and communication expertise.

This report has highlighted a number of practices – some current, others aspirational – which constitute a manifesto for twenty-first-century corporate security.

Philosophy for security

Corporate security departments must:

○ 'let go' – they cannot deliver security to the rest of the organisation and must be committed to the idea of commitment-based security; they understand that their authority and legitimacy come from openness and transparency rather than secrecy, and work hard to break dispel the 'security myth'

○ not practise the 'dark art of security' – they should not overreact to 'security moments' or use them cynically as opportunities to fight for more resources or authority, nor seek to play others' lack of knowledge to their own advantage

○ be driven by business priorities – from new organising principles, such as corporate governance, to new business practices, such as offshoring

○ not look for Rolls-Royce solutions – absolute security is

not possible anywhere, and is certainly not desirable in a
corporate setting where the economic imperative is key

O   place a premium on good relationships – both within the
company and between the company and its stakeholders;
fortress security can lose a company friends as well as
harming the bottom line

O   understand the importance of communication – they
must work hard to sell their services, gain visibility across
the company, influence key decision-makers and challenge
misperceptions, where necessary.

Group security department

Departments must:

O   expand their work far beyond the traditional security
portfolio to include issues such as business continuity,
reputation, risk management and corporate
responsibility; this creates added pressure to manage
across, emphasising the importance of networks and
change management skills

O   have as short a reporting line to the board as possible

O   act as a key point of coordination for corporate security
(in the widest sense) across the company

O   embrace changes to the internal and external
environments

O   understand that there is still more work to be done in
aligning security with the business through, for example,
strategic plans, metrics that measure the work of the
department against the strategic priorities of the business,
and more formal links with other parts of the business
(for example appraisal processes).

Head of security

Heads of security must:

O   be effective leaders – they should be credible players

alongside peers at the top of their companies and have democratic and open styles of leadership within their own teams

O   occupy senior positions within their companies

O   have regular contact with their boards and senior management teams and invest significant time in raising awareness of security among the board members

O   work at a strategic rather than tactical level; be presentation-led rather than content-led

O   view their security experience as being far less important than their business, management and communications experience

O   encourage and facilitate relationships between their department and staff right across the company.

Security team

Security teams must:

O   value diversity – gender, age, ethnicity, leadership styles and core competencies

O   place a premium on business skills

O   understand the importance of investing far more time and resources on the mechanisms for change – personnel development, fast-track schemes for security professionals, rotation and developing qualifications.

Organisational structure

Corporate security departments must be committed to business integration, and will achieve this through a number of means, such as:

O   sitting on key committees and working groups that link them into other areas of the business or give them influence at a senior level

O   being committed to alignment with the project management and coordination process

O developing a variety of reporting structures, with an understanding of the importance of 'structural layering'

O delegating as much responsibility as possible for security from group level to the business unit

O valuing the regional layer, but acknowledging that it is difficult to get right; developing innovative responses, such as 'cluster security' models

O having small central budgets, with the bulk of budgets decentralised to the business units.

Notes

1   N Nohria and TA Stewart, 'Risk, uncertainty and doubt, the HBR list, breakthrough ideas for 2006', *Harvard Business Review* (Feb 2006).
2   *Business Security Survey 2004*, MORI, IPSOS and the Confederation of British Industry (CBI) in association with QinetiQ.
3   Ibid.
4   TE Cavanagh, *Corporate Security Measures and Practices: An overview of security management since 9/11* (New York: The Conference Board, 2005).
5   Ibid.
6   *Business Security Survey 2004*.
7   Link Associates International, *Information & Communications Survey Report: 7th July 2005* (Derby: Link Associates International, nd), see www.thebci.org/7-7Report.pdf (accessed 31 May 2006).
8   J Flynn, P Slovic and H Kunreuther, *Risk, Media and Stigma: Understanding public challenges to modern science and technology* (London: Earthscan, 2001).
9   WK Viscusi, 'Alarmist decisions with divergent risk information', *Economic Journal* 107, no 445 (1997).
10 *Business Security Survey 2004*.
11 AR Ciancutti and TL Steding, *Built on Trust: Gaining competitive advantage in any organization* (Burr Ridge, IL: McGraw-Hill Education, 2001).
12 Institute of Chartered Accountants, *Internal Control: Guidance for directors on the Combined Code* (the Turnbull Report), (London: The Institute of Chartered Accountants in England & Wales, Sep 1999).
13 The Sarbanes-Oxley Act of 2002 (Pub. L. No. 107-204, 116 Stat. 745), known as the Public Company Accounting Reform and Investor Protection Act of 2002.
14 Basel Committee on Banking Supervision, *Basel II: International Convergence of Capital Measurement and Capital Standards: a revised framework* (Basel: Basel Committee on Banking Supervision, Nov 2005).
15 Booz Allen Hamilton, *Convergence of Enterprise Security Organizations* (Booz Allen Hamilton, Nov 2005), see www.boozallen.com (accessed 1 Jun 2006).
16 Cavanagh, *Corporate Security Measures and Practices*.

17 K van Brabant, *Security and Humanitarian Space: Perspective of an aid agency* (Bochum: Humanitares Volkerrecht, 1998).

18 Cited in R Holme and P Watts, *Corporate Social Responsibility: Making good business sense* (Tockwith, UK: World Business Council for Sustainable Development, Jan 2000).

19 Overseas Development Institute and Pro-Poor Tourism Pilots, 'Doing business differently in tourism', 23 May 2005, see www.pptpilot.org.za/ppt_workshop/ppt_report/index.html (accessed 31 May 2006).

20 For definitions of 'outsourcing' and 'offshoring' see www.fsa.org.uk or http://en.wikipedia.org/wiki/Offshoring (both accessed 31 May 2006).

21 B Dudley, 'US economics analyst', *Goldman-Sachs Newsletter* 38 (Sep 2003).

22 T Sanders, 'Gartner warns of offshore ID theft risk', *vnunet.com*, 13 Sep 2005, see www.vnunet.com/vnunet/news/2142204/gartner-warns-indian-call (accessed 31 May 2006).

23 V Agrawal et al, 'Offshoring and beyond: cheap labour is the beginning not the end', *McKinsey Quarterly*, special edn (2003).

24 Deloitte, *The Titans Take Hold: How offshoring has changed the competitive dynamic for global financial services institutions*, research report (Deloitte, 2004), see www.deloitte.com/dtt/research/ 0,1015,sid%253D15288%2526cid%253D51146,00.html (accessed 2 Jun 2006).

25 See www.pharmabiz.com/article/detnews.asp?SecArch =s&articleid= 16090&sectionid=42 (accessed 5 Jun 2006, subscription needed for full story).

26 See G Gause III, 'Can democracy stop terrorism?', *Foreign Affairs*, Sep/Oct 2005.

27 R Lal, 'Terrorism in India is not just an internal threat', *Financial Times*, 30 Sep 2003.

28 Financial Services Authority, *Offshore Operations: Industry feedback* (London: FSA, Apr 2005).

29 Ibid.

30 J Oates, 'India acts on call centre fraud', *The Register Online*, 13 Apr 2005.

31 Ibid.

32 FSA, *Offshore Operations*.

33 Deloitte, *Titans Take Hold*.

34 For further discussion on this theme, see R Briggs, 'Perception gap: public attitudes to security and their impact on policy-making and corporate decision-making' in R Briggs, *Joining Forces: From national security to networked security* (London: Demos, 2005).

35 See http://topics.developmentgateway.org (accessed 7 Jun 2006).

36 FSA, *Offshore Operations*.

37 'Customers "concerned" over offshoring of banking operations', Forensic & Litigation Services, KPMG Forensic (press release), 27 Sep 2005.

38 Dan Hooton, 'Analysing the role of the corporate security function in an organisation: what are the major influences on today's security manager?', unpublished dissertation, University of Portsmouth, 2005.

39 See http://courses.chalkface.com/public_html/encyc/U2M02-

03Functional.html (accessed 31 May 2006).

40   See www.pmforum.org/library/papers/2003/youkerorgalt.pdf (accessed 31 May 2006).

41   See for example SR Davis and PR Lawrence, *Matrix* (Reading, MA: Addison Wesley, 1978); RC Ford and WA Randolph, 'Cross-functional structures: a review and integration of matrix organization and project management', *Journal of Management* 18, no 2 (1992); T Hayhoe, 'Making matrix structures work' (nd), see www.brackenbury.co.uk/making_matrix_structures_work.htm (accessed 7 Jun 2006); and C Albano, 'Functional, project and matrix structures' (nd), see www.leader-values.com/content/detail.asp?ContentDetailID=958 (accessed 7 Jun 2006).

42   Cavanagh, *Corporate Security Measures and Practices*.

43   Ibid.

44   D Burrill, 'Corporate security: past, present and future', presentation to Demos, see www.demos.co.uk/projects/joiningforces (accessed 5 Jun 2006).

45   S Berinato, 'Value made visible: how American Water's Bruce Larson uses a simple metric to build bridges with business partners and justify security spending at the same time', *CSO Online*, 1 Apr 2006, see www.csoonline.com/read/040106/value_visible.html (accessed 31 May 2006).

46   Ibid.

47   J Chapman, *System Failure*, 2nd edn (London: Demos, 2004).

48   See R Cross and A Parker, *The Hidden Power of Social Networks: Understanding how work really gets done in organisations* (Boston, MA: Harvard Business School Press, 2004).

49   Ibid.

50   Ibid.

51   Ibid.

52   See A Shapiro, *Creating Contagious Commitment: Applying the tipping point to organisational change* (Hillsborough, NC: Strategy Perspective, 2003).

53   Ibid.

54   Burrill, 'Corporate security'.

55   M Armstrong Whiting and TE Cavanagh, *Corporate Security Management: Organization and spending since 9/11* (New York: The Conference Board, Jul 2003).

56   'Executive salary survey', SSR Personnel, for more details see www.ssr-personnel.com (accessed 7 Jun 2006).

57   R Briggs, 'Hidden assets: putting people at the heart of security' in *Joining Forces*.

58   E Borodzicz, 'Security and risk: a new approach to managing loss prevention', *International Journal of Risk, Security and Crime Prevention* 1, no 2 (1996).

59   See Borodzicz, 'Security and risk' and Briggs, 'Perception gap'.

60   SSR Personnel.

61   Briggs, 'Hidden assets'.

62   See www.computerworld.com/printthis/2001/0,4814,61965,00.html (accessed 7 Jun 2006).

63   ASIS International, *Chief Security Officer (CSO) Guideline* (2004), available at www.asisonline.org/guidelines/guidelineschief.pdf (accessed 5 Jun 2006).

64   See http://en.wikipedia.org/wiki/Leadership#Suggested_qualities_of_leadership (accessed 1 Jun 2006).

65   See http://ut.essortment.com/leadershipstyle_rrnq.htm (accessed 1 Jun 2006).

66   See http://bama.ua.edu/~st497/pdf/creatingteamleaders.pdf (accessed 1 Jun 2006).

67   See http://ut.essortment.com/leadershipstyle_rrnq.htm (accessed 1 Jun 2006).

68   See www.see.ed.ac.uk/~gerard/MENG/ME96/Documents/Styles/styles.html#lais (accessed 1 Jun 2006).

69   K Carr, 'Feather your nest', *CSO Online* (Jun 2004), see www.csoonline.com/read/060104/feather.html (accessed 7 Jun 2006).

70   See www.csocouncil.org (accessed 7 Jun 2006).

71   ASIS International, *Chief Security Officer (CSO) Guideline.*

72   See www.skillsforsecurity.org.uk (accessed 5 Jun 2006).

73   ASIS International, *Chief Security Officer (CSO) Guideline.*

DEMOS – Licence to Publish

THE WORK (AS DEFINED BELOW) IS PROVIDED UNDER THE TERMS OF THIS LICENCE ("LICENCE"). THE
WORK IS PROTECTED BY COPYRIGHT AND/OR OTHER APPLICABLE LAW. ANY USE OF THE WORK OTHER
THAN AS AUTHORIZED UNDER THIS LICENCE IS PROHIBITED. BY EXERCISING ANY RIGHTS TO THE WORK
PROVIDED HERE, YOU ACCEPT AND AGREE TO BE BOUND BY THE TERMS OF THIS LICENCE. DEMOS
GRANTS YOU THE RIGHTS CONTAINED HERE IN CONSIDERATION OF YOUR ACCEPTANCE OF SUCH TERMS
AND CONDITIONS.

1. **Definitions**
   a **"Collective Work"** means a work, such as a periodical issue, anthology or encyclopedia, in which
   the Work in its entirety in unmodified form, along with a number of other contributions,
   constituting separate and independent works in themselves, are assembled into a collective
   whole. A work that constitutes a Collective Work will not be considered a Derivative Work (as
   defined below) for the purposes of this Licence.
   b **"Derivative Work"** means a work based upon the Work or upon the Work and other pre-existing
   works, such as a musical arrangement, dramatization, fictionalization, motion picture version,
   sound recording, art reproduction, abridgment, condensation, or any other form in which the
   Work may be recast, transformed, or adapted, except that a work that constitutes a Collective
   Work or a translation from English into another language will not be considered a Derivative
   Work for the purpose of this Licence.
   c **"Licensor"** means the individual or entity that offers the Work under the terms of this Licence.
   d **"Original Author"** means the individual or entity who created the Work.
   e **"Work"** means the copyrightable work of authorship offered under the terms of this Licence.
   f **"You"** means an individual or entity exercising rights under this Licence who has not previously
   violated the terms of this Licence with respect to the Work, or who has received express permission
   from DEMOS to exercise rights under this Licence despite a previous violation.
2. **Fair Use Rights.** Nothing in this licence is intended to reduce, limit, or restrict any rights arising from
   fair use, first sale or other limitations on the exclusive rights of the copyright owner under copyright
   law or other applicable laws.
3. **Licence Grant.** Subject to the terms and conditions of this Licence, Licensor hereby grants You a
   worldwide, royalty-free, non-exclusive, perpetual (for the duration of the applicable copyright) licence
   to exercise the rights in the Work as stated below:
   a to reproduce the Work, to incorporate the Work into one or more Collective Works, and to
   reproduce the Work as incorporated in the Collective Works;
   b to distribute copies or phonorecords of, display publicly, perform publicly, and perform publicly
   by means of a digital audio transmission the Work including as incorporated in Collective Works;
   The above rights may be exercised in all media and formats whether now known or hereafter
   devised. The above rights include the right to make such modifications as are technically necessary to
   exercise the rights in other media and formats. All rights not expressly granted by Licensor are hereby
   reserved.
4. **Restrictions.** The licence granted in Section 3 above is expressly made subject to and limited by the
   following restrictions:
   a You may distribute, publicly display, publicly perform, or publicly digitally perform the Work only
   under the terms of this Licence, and You must include a copy of, or the Uniform Resource
   Identifier for, this Licence with every copy or phonorecord of the Work You distribute, publicly
   display, publicly perform, or publicly digitally perform. You may not offer or impose any terms on
   the Work that alter or restrict the terms of this Licence or the recipients' exercise of the rights
   granted hereunder. You may not sublicence the Work. You must keep intact all notices that refer
   to this Licence and to the disclaimer of warranties. You may not distribute, publicly display,
   publicly perform, or publicly digitally perform the Work with any technological measures that
   control access or use of the Work in a manner inconsistent with the terms of this Licence
   Agreement. The above applies to the Work as incorporated in a Collective Work, but this does not
   require the Collective Work apart from the Work itself to be made subject to the terms of this
   Licence. If You create a Collective Work, upon notice from any Licencor You must, to the extent
   practicable, remove from the Collective Work any reference to such Licensor or the Original
   Author, as requested.
   b You may not exercise any of the rights granted to You in Section 3 above in any manner that is
   primarily intended for or directed toward commercial advantage or private monetary

compensation. The exchange of the Work for other copyrighted works by means of digital file-sharing or otherwise shall not be considered to be intended for or directed toward commercial advantage or private monetary compensation, provided there is no payment of any monetary compensation in connection with the exchange of copyrighted works.

  c If you distribute, publicly display, publicly perform, or publicly digitally perform the Work or any Collective Works, You must keep intact all copyright notices for the Work and give the Original Author credit reasonable to the medium or means You are utilizing by conveying the name (or pseudonym if applicable) of the Original Author if supplied; the title of the Work if supplied. Such credit may be implemented in any reasonable manner; provided, however, that in the case of a Collective Work, at a minimum such credit will appear where any other comparable authorship credit appears and in a manner at least as prominent as such other comparable authorship credit.

5. Representations, Warranties and Disclaimer

  a By offering the Work for public release under this Licence, Licensor represents and warrants that, to the best of Licensor's knowledge after reasonable inquiry:

    i Licensor has secured all rights in the Work necessary to grant the licence rights hereunder and to permit the lawful exercise of the rights granted hereunder without You having any obligation to pay any royalties, compulsory licence fees, residuals or any other payments;

    ii The Work does not infringe the copyright, trademark, publicity rights, common law rights or any other right of any third party or constitute defamation, invasion of privacy or other tortious injury to any third party.

  b EXCEPT AS EXPRESSLY STATED IN THIS LICENCE OR OTHERWISE AGREED IN WRITING OR REQUIRED BY APPLICABLE LAW, THE WORK IS LICENCED ON AN "AS IS" BASIS, WITHOUT WARRANTIES OF ANY KIND, EITHER EXPRESS OR IMPLIED INCLUDING, WITHOUT LIMITATION, ANY WARRANTIES REGARDING THE CONTENTS OR ACCURACY OF THE WORK.

6. Limitation on Liability. EXCEPT TO THE EXTENT REQUIRED BY APPLICABLE LAW, AND EXCEPT FOR DAMAGES ARISING FROM LIABILITY TO A THIRD PARTY RESULTING FROM BREACH OF THE WARRANTIES IN SECTION 5, IN NO EVENT WILL LICENSOR BE LIABLE TO YOU ON ANY LEGAL THEORY FOR ANY SPECIAL, INCIDENTAL, CONSEQUENTIAL, PUNITIVE OR EXEMPLARY DAMAGES ARISING OUT OF THIS LICENCE OR THE USE OF THE WORK, EVEN IF LICENSOR HAS BEEN ADVISED OF THE POSSIBILITY OF SUCH DAMAGES.

7. Termination

  a This Licence and the rights granted hereunder will terminate automatically upon any breach by You of the terms of this Licence. Individuals or entities who have received Collective Works from You under this Licence, however, will not have their licences terminated provided such individuals or entities remain in full compliance with those licences. Sections 1, 2, 5, 6, 7, and 8 will survive any termination of this Licence.

  b Subject to the above terms and conditions, the licence granted here is perpetual (for the duration of the applicable copyright in the Work). Notwithstanding the above, Licensor reserves the right to release the Work under different licence terms or to stop distributing the Work at any time; provided, however that any such election will not serve to withdraw this Licence (or any other licence that has been, or is required to be, granted under the terms of this Licence), and this Licence will continue in full force and effect unless terminated as stated above.

8. Miscellaneous

  a Each time You distribute or publicly digitally perform the Work or a Collective Work, DEMOS offers to the recipient a licence to the Work on the same terms and conditions as the licence granted to You under this Licence.

  b If any provision of this Licence is invalid or unenforceable under applicable law, it shall not affect the validity or enforceability of the remainder of the terms of this Licence, and without further action by the parties to this agreement, such provision shall be reformed to the minimum extent necessary to make such provision valid and enforceable.

  c No term or provision of this Licence shall be deemed waived and no breach consented to unless such waiver or consent shall be in writing and signed by the party to be charged with such waiver or consent.

  d This Licence constitutes the entire agreement between the parties with respect to the Work licensed here. There are no understandings, agreements or representations with respect to the Work not specified here. Licensor shall not be bound by any additional provisions that may appear in any communication from You. This Licence may not be modified without the mutual written agreement of DEMOS and You.